The New Learning Centre
Skills for Success at School and Harmony in the Home

211 Sumatra Road, London NW6 1PF
Tel: 020 7794 0321   Fax: 020 7431 8600
admin@tnlc.info   www.tnlc.info
Director: Noël Janis-Norton

Could Do Better ...

How Parents can Help their Children Succeed at School

Noël Janis-Norton

Barrington Stoke

First published in Great Britain by Barrington Stoke Ltd,
Sandeman House, 55 High Street, Edinburgh, EH1 1SR

www.barringtonstoke.co.uk

ISBN 1-84299-303-8

Edited by Julia Rowlandson
Cover design by Kate MacPhee
Typeset by GreenGate Publishing Services, Tonbridge, TN9 2RN
Printed in Great Britain by The Cromwell Press

CONTENTS

Acknowledgements

Many wise individuals and innovative organisations have enriched my work with families and schools. In addition to all my colleagues at The New Learning Centre, past and present, I would like to acknowledge:

Alfred Adler	Landmark EducationApplied
Behavioural Analysis	Phil McGraw
Tony Buzan	Maria Montessori
Julia Cameron	Neuro-Linguistic Programming
Dale Carnegie	Psychology of Vision
Dalai Lama	Jane Ross and Lee Janis
Rudoph Dreikurs	Barbara Sher
Haim Ginott	Son-rise Programme
Thomas Gordon	Benjamin Spock
John Gray	Twelve-Step Programmes
John Holt	Marianne Williamson
Susan Jeffers	Phyllis and David York

My profound gratitude to my dear friends – you know who are you – for your love, encouragement and belief in me.

Special thanks to all The New Learning Centre parents, whose honesty, enthusiasm for new ideas and determination to create calmer, easier, happier families continues to inspire me and give me hope for the future.

My deepest appreciation to my children, Jessica, Jordan and Chloe for their unstinting love and support, and to my grandchildren Shaun, Anna, Cameron, Alexander and Zoey, for reminding me, again and again, of the potential of the human spirit.

This book is dedicated to all parents who are searching for ways to help their children be, and feel, more successful.

SECTION I: Partners in education: Parents, pupils and teachers

CHAPTER 1

What we mean by "school success", and why it matters so much

As parents, we want our children to fulfil their potential. We want to help our children to achieve everything that they are capable of achieving. And for most children, a large part of the achievement that parents hope for is "doing well" at school.

Parents have numerous reasons for wanting their children to do as well as they possibly can at school. Parents know that school success matters because:

- Children are naturally happier and more enthusiastic about life when their innate abilities are being fully used and stretched.
- Competence leads to confidence.
- The skills and habits learned at school will be very useful in later life, in the areas of further or higher education, work, relationships and leisure.
- School is a child's "job", and society takes this job very seriously. Parents, relatives and even strangers ask:
    "How's school?"
    "What are you studying?"
    "How's your reading (or maths) coming along?"
    Rightly or wrongly, a child is often judged, and soon comes to judge himself, according to his academic performance. Peers, also, notice and talk about school success and lack of success. When a child is not enjoying his "job" or consistently not doing well, he does not have the option, as we do, of switching jobs.

We know that children do not all learn in the same way. Just as children differ in their physical appearance, their brains also differ. Some children

quickly understand and easily remember what they are taught, while others need much more repetition. Some always gravitate towards reading fiction; others will choose only factual books. Some are curious and eager to engage with schoolwork, while others of the same age just want to be left alone to play.

Of course we can easily see the colour of a child's eyes or whether he is short or tall. But we cannot look inside a child's mind when we want to find out what kind of brain he has. So when we are trying to discover what our child's brain is capable of, we tend to look at his schoolwork, comparing his academic performance against that of the other pupils in his class. Or we think back to when his siblings, or we ourselves, were his age. But these comparisons cannot fully tell us what our child's brain is capable of because there are several factors which influence how well a child will do at school. One of these influences is the child's innate genetic inheritance, and another is the child's environment, both at home and at school.

Many parents worry because they do not know how to bring out the best in their children. We have all seen how even a very bright child can drift into becoming an under-achiever if he is not guided to develop good habits and sound basic skills. One distraught, confused father commented, "I don't have a clue how to help my son get back on track. It feels like my wife and I are sitting helplessly on the sidelines as our boy digs himself deeper and deeper into bad habits."

Conversely, a child who finds learning or concentrating more difficult can *be successful, and feel successful* if he receives the teaching and training that is right for his kind of brain. A child or teenager who has been taught efficient "school success skills" knows how to learn and therefore enjoys learning more. He has the tools to fulfil his brain's potential. If his potential is very high, we can expect him to master knowledge and skills at a high level. If his potential is more limited, he will find the learning process harder, slower or more frustrating. He may never be an academic high-flyer, but he can still fulfil his own potential.

A child with efficient school success skills has a tool kit which includes:

- The basic academic skills of listening
  Speaking
  Reading
  Writing
  Numeracy
- Positive attitudes (which are also skills), e.g.
  Enthusiasm
  Motivation
  Co-operation
  Curiosity
  Confidence
  Self-reliance
  Self-control
  Doing one's best
  Attention to detail
  Perseverance
  Patience
  Consideration

These are all skills that can be learned. And it is the job of parents, not of teachers, to make sure that our children learn them and then practise them until they are habitual. With these tools, any child can achieve his potential.

You have noticed, I am sure, that I have been writing about your child as "he" and "him". I will do this throughout the book because boys make up more than three-quarters of all children who have problems with attention, learning and behaviour.

CHAPTER 2

Why schools by themselves cannot help all pupils to fulfil their potential

There are several important reasons why parents cannot sit back and just expect teachers to do the job of training children in those important school success skills.

1   A great deal of research has been done about learning styles (strengths and weaknesses). Researchers know much more than they did even ten years ago about the relative effectiveness of different teaching styles. We now know, in theory, how to help *every child* to achieve his potential! But it can take a long time for research findings to become a reality in the classroom.

2   Teachers are exposed to new teaching methods mostly through in-service training. This is often delivered by lecturers who have not had recent experience of the harsh realities of the classroom. Without intending to, these lecturers may paint an unrealistic picture and imply that the new strategies will be easy to put into practice. The initial response of teachers to hearing about new strategies may be enthusiasm and excitement. But this can quickly sour because teachers are often expected to implement new ideas based on a one-day course, and without effective, consistent support from their senior management team. Because of this, many useful strategies fall by the wayside. And teachers often end up feeling disillusioned.

3   Even when teachers do understand what a particular child needs in order to fulfil his potential, schools may not able to provide what is needed, due to a shortage of funding. For example, in almost every classroom there will be a few children who need a very different kind of learning environment. They need individual, skilled instruction and

very quiet, purposeful, calm surroundings. These pupils may be too distractible, too self-conscious or too easily upset to stay focused on their work in a busy, noisy classroom.

Even pupils with an acknowledged, assessed learning disability and an official "statement of special educational needs" are likely to be receiving only a small fraction of what they would need in order to *really* achieve what they are capable of achieving.

4   Any pupil who is experiencing difficulties will learn more successfully and feel more confident (and as a consequence also behave more maturely) when he is given plenty of time to master a topic or skill before having to move on to the next level of difficulty. A great deal of schoolwork is sequential. Each new skill is best learned when it is built on a solid foundation of previously-mastered skills and information. When a pupil has not mastered certain basic skills and facts, any subsequent learning will be like building on sand. The structure is bound to be shaky.

It is easy to understand why teachers move the whole class on as soon as the majority of the pupils have shown that they are ready. The needs of the majority who are coping and learning outweigh the needs of the few who are struggling. But some children in every class need lessons that progress at a much slower pace and that include much more repetition and more hands-on active participation at each stage of learning.

A national policy of differentiation was introduced in an attempt to ensure that all pupils are always working at the level that is just right for them. Differentiation means adjusting the work so that each pupil can learn. Work can be differentiated in numerous ways, e.g. by level, by the amount a pupil is expected to do, by the time allowed, or by how the work is presented.

Effective differentiation is often not easy to implement. It can take a lot of the teacher's time, and it requires good organisation. The support available to organise differentiation effectively varies from school to school.

Differentiation solves some problems, but like most solutions, it often creates a new set of problems. Some children feel embarrassed and

demoralised when given obviously easier work. And even with differentiation, a significant minority of pupils are still left behind, not quite understanding, not quite remembering, and definitely not fulfilling their potential. Over time the gap in attainment between pupils in the same year continues to widen.

5   No teacher, no matter how gifted or dedicated, will ever care about a child's success as much as the parents do.

Schools accept that in any given classroom only a few pupils (those commonly labelled "quick, bright, able, intelligent") will excel, most pupils will perform adequately, and a few pupils will continually struggle with learning.

A pupil who rarely experiences success will, over time, lose confidence and enthusiasm. He may begin to think of himself as a failure and a disappointment. Eventually he may even give up trying. So it is not at all surprising that these same pupils continue to scrape along the bottom of the class, year after year. No parents are happy for their child to be among the group of children who continue to feel unsuccessful.

6   Teachers may have a one-sided view of a child who is experiencing problems at school. They are not able to see all the areas, outside of school, where he functions adequately or possibly even shines. Therefore, the teachers of a pupil who continually struggles with learning may conclude that the child is in fact achieving his potential but that unfortunately his potential is quite low.

Living with the child and seeing him in many different situations, parents are in a much better position to see his true potential. They are also in an ideal position to help their child do and be their best. These children need what schools often cannot provide:

- More individual instruction from an adult who understands about learning differences.
- More time to take in and absorb the information they need to learn.

- More frequent feedback, especially feedback about what they are doing right, so that they can build on their strengths.
- More practice (including practice at evaluating their own work).
- A calmer, quieter, more orderly learning environment.

The solution is not to waste time blaming the school or complaining but to take charge and provide at home what your child needs but may not be getting from school.

CHAPTER 3

Why parents need to take charge of their children's education, what that really means, and what it can achieve

When pupils are taught the vital school success skills, they are finally able, for the first time in their school lives, to fulfil their potential. They learn what they are capable of learning, and they apply what they have learned. Their curiosity, enthusiasm and self-confidence blossom, and they enjoy their "job". This is what parents want for their children. This is what every child deserves.

You may feel very strongly that your child's school should provide what he needs. Of course that is true. You may want to do something to make that happen. You can work to help your school help your child more effectively. You can even make suggestions about how to improve the whole school system. But don't hold your breath waiting for systems to change. Reforms usually happen very slowly, and in the meantime your child may be missing out, possibly even suffering.

Instead of complaining or resigning yourself to an unsatisfactory situation, take action. You, the parent, can provide what the child needs in order to become a successful learner.

> **Our children's education is far too important to leave up to the schools**

Thinking in this way helps parents to feel positive, rather than discouraged, when they or their children encounter some of the inevitable problems associated with schooling.

Some parents will choose to be the sole educators of their children, but that is not what suits most modern families. What I am suggesting is that parents see themselves as the most important educators of their children, not necessarily as the only educators.

There are many superb resources available, both within and outside of school. Parents need to inform themselves so that they can assess carefully, monitor thoroughly, liaise assertively yet diplomatically, and advocate relentlessly (see Appendix B for information about advocacy). Taking charge of our children's education means taking on the *full responsibility* for managing our children's experience of school so that they get the most out of school.

The steps to taking charge are:

1 Parents clarify their goals for each child, deciding what he will need, from home and from school, in order to fulfil his potential, to thrive academically, behaviourally and socially. Whenever possible, both parents working as a team need to decide on these goals.
2 Together, parents plan how to achieve these goals, i.e. how to meet each child's educational needs.
3 Together, parents put their well-thought-out plans into action, and follow through until they see the desired results.

There are several key features to the "School Success Skills" programme:

- It is, of course, the teachers' responsibility to teach the school subjects. The parents' role, however, is just as important. Our job as parents is to prepare our child, to enable him to access and take advantage of everything the school has to offer. To achieve this we will need to take on the responsibility for teaching and training the all-important "school success skills".
- We will also need to teach and train our child in the life skills that help develop self-reliance and self-confidence.

- We need to stay aware, day by day, of what is happening at school and how our child is responding.
- Parents need to be advocates for their children, supporting them and working with the school (see *Communicating effectively with with your child's school*, at the end of this chapter – page 25).
- We will need to closely supervise the daily homework time so that we establish productive, enjoyable homework habits (see Section III).
- We will need to fill in the gaps when the curriculum moves too fast, leaving our child behind.
- We need to learn about and practise new ways of communicating with and disciplining our children so that they become more and more co-operative, confident, motivated, self-reliant and considerate (see Section III).
- Most difficult of all, we will probably need to change the family's lifestyle in order to give each child the best possible chance to be, and feel, successful (see Section IV).

The above to-do list may seem daunting. You may be worried that you lack the patience, the education or the free time to take charge of your child's education. However, this programme does not require you to invest any more time supervising homework than you normally would. Instead it asks you to *do things differently within the daily homework time*. You do not need to remember much of what you learned at school because your job is not to teach subject matter. Your job will be to train your child in good habits. And as you put the parenting skills into practice, you will find that you need much less patience because you will encounter a lot less resistance or negativity and a lot more co-operation and enthusiasm.

Homework and home learning are important keys to school success

The usual advice that parents are given about helping children to do well at school is useful as far as it goes:

- Make sure that your child has a desk in a quiet, well-lighted area.

- Give him access to an appropriate dictionary and reference materials (see Appendix B).
- Show an interest.
- Make sure he sees you reading.
- Go to all parents' evenings.

As useful as this basic advice may be, it is not enough! Many parents who have followed these suggestions are still worried because their children are not doing their best, either at school or with their homework. Consequently, these children are not learning what they could and should be learning, both in terms of school subjects and of good habits.

The parents of these children and teenagers are frustrated and want to know what else they can do. Luckily, there are alternatives to letting the schoolwork and homework situation deteriorate until it becomes a huge source of tension in the family.

Homework is the one aspect of their children's schooling that parents have the most access to and the most influence over. Therefore, it makes sense for parents to be pro-active and to harness the huge potential of homework to improve academic learning and sensible work habits.

One could debate the relative merits of different types of homework, or even the value of homework per se, but that is not my brief. I want to help children and teens to feel successful. In schools where homework is set, most young people cannot be (or feel) successful unless they are handing their homework in on time and *doing their best* on their homework. And even when children are attending schools that do not set homework, I still always recommend that some formal academic home learning, targeted to the child's specific needs, be done daily.

I believe that regardless of ability or skill level, all children need to do homework because

- all children have weak areas that need to be strengthened
- all children should be stretched, and parents can do this better than teachers can because parents know the children better and because they can work one-to-one with each child

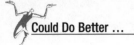

- all children need to develop good work habits and become more and more self-reliant.

In Section III I will show, in step-by-step detail, how you can use the daily homework sessions to transform a relatively negative situation into a positive one.

Here are the basics of the School Success Skills programme:

Who *will do it?*

This programme requires your active participation every day. On days when you are not available, you will need to ask another adult to stand in.

What *will you be doing?*

Six days a week (including holidays) you will be closely supervising all your child's home learning. There are two categories of home learning:

a Homework, reading, memorising, revision and projects
b Life skills – this means being able to take care of himself: hygiene, public transport, food preparation, household tasks, shopping and banking, etc.

Where *will you be doing this?*

a At home, in a hotel room if you are on holiday, wherever you and your child happen to be during the sacred homework hour.
b The teaching of life skills takes place in the kitchen, at the park, at the supermarket, the cinema, Scouts, karate or piano lessons, church or a grandparent's home, wherever you and your child are together.

When *will you do this?*

a Your participation will be needed for one hour every day during the usual homework time. For younger children the hour can be divided into two separate half-hours or even three sessions of twenty minutes each.
b The life skills teaching will happen whenever you and your children are together.

How *will you do this?*

a During the daily homework time you will establish routines and habits that will make homework productive and enjoyable.

b You will be on the lookout for the little life lessons your child can be learning all day long, so that you can influence him in the direction of the skills, values and habits that matter to you.

How *will you do this?*

You need to take charge of your children's homework habits and life skills because these are the school success skills that will enhance learning, boost confidence and motivation, and enable your children to get the most from school and from all the other areas of their lives. Homework habits lead to school habits, which lead to life habits.

Most educators acknowledge that children forget a vast amount of what they learn at school. As adults, we generally have only a vague recollection of topics such as the Tudors, ancient Egypt, the Greek gods, photosynthesis, strong and weak verbs, quadratic equations, etc. What most often remains, after we have forgotten many of the details of the subjects we studied, are the skills of literacy and numeracy, a great deal of "general knowledge" and certain positive attitudes and mature habits, such as enthusiasm, perseverance, attention to detail and problem-solving. These are the basic skills and habits that enable adults to be employable and to function adequately in many other areas of life, including relationships and leisure pursuits.

I am not suggesting that parents and teachers should focus solely on literacy and numeracy at the expense of history, science, geography, art, music, P.E., etc. Those subjects are intrinsically important for many reasons. And those subjects can be exciting vehicles for the learning of literacy, numeracy and positive attitudes and habits.

What exactly are the academic skills and the positive attitudes that all children need to master in order to be, and feel, successful? As you read through the following list of basic skills, you may protest that you want your child to end up knowing much more than this. Children who are academically able will, of course, progress beyond this basic level. Here I

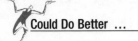

am outlining the ground-floor level that will give your child access to the higher levels.

Literacy

1. Reading

a. Decoding & reading aloud – your child should be able to:

- know which letters and letter combinations make which sounds. This is known as synthetic phonics and in English is initially quite difficult for many children to master because our language has 44 sounds but only 26 letters. As a result, many letters and letter combinations make more than one sound (*c*ity, *c*an; enough, though, ought). To confuse matters further, many sounds are represented by more than one letter (*c*at, *k*itten) or combination of letters (*si*ght, *si*te).
- read (in isolation as well as in context) any syllable that is composed of phonetically regular elements (e.g. *lem, ver, tran*)
- recognise instantly and pronounce correctly words with consonant clusters (e.g. *spl, str, gh, thr*)
- correctly read words with vowel blends (e.g. *au, ou, oi*)
- correctly read words with long vowel sounds (e.g. silent *e, oa, ea, ee, igh*)
- recognise instantly all of the sight words on the list of the 220 most commonly used words (see Appendix A).
- blend sounds smoothly when sounding out unfamiliar words
- read aloud smoothly and with expression:
    - the voice goes down for full stops
    - the voice goes up for questions
    - the voice is more animated for exclamation marks
    - slight pause at commas
    - emphasise the important words in each sentence.
- read silently without:
    - pointing to each word
    - whispering
    - moving head
    - moving lips.

Mastery of these basic reading skills will free up your child's attention to concentrate on the meaning and relevance of what he is reading.

b. Reading comprehension – your child should be able to:

- Correct himself in mid-sentence, and re-read the whole sentence correctly, if a decoding mistake results in the sentence not making sense.
- Understand the meaning of common expressions and idioms, e.g.
  - It was raining cats and dogs
  - They ate us out of house and home
  - She flew down the stairs.
- Correctly answer questions that demonstrate his ability to recall and understand
  - a sequence of events
  - the reasons why characters do certain things
  - the significance of key details.
- Predict, deduce and infer.
- Make up, and then answer, questions about a book or passage.
- Consult reference materials to clarify meanings (see Appendix B).

2. Writing

a. Composing sentences and paragraphs – your child should be able to:

- Write in complete sentences, not fragments.
- Define (explain clearly what something is).
- Narrate (relate events or steps in the correct sequence).
- Use adjectives and adverbs to describe more fully and precisely.
- Write a short paragraph consisting of a topic sentence stating the main point of what he wants to say, followed by 3–5 sentences which support the first sentence (either by describing in detail, giving examples, giving reasons, etc.) and a concluding sentence, briefly summing up.
- Write from dictation accurately.
- Copy exactly (or learn an alternative coping strategy).

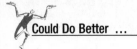

b. Vocabulary – your child should be able to:

- Paraphrase (put ideas in his own words).
- Use more descriptive verbs, rather than *got, had, did*.
- Use more descriptive adjectives, rather than *nice, fun, awful*.
- Choose the appropriate word to convey a precise meaning (e.g. *shed, hut, cabin* or *vacant, empty, abandoned*).
- Avoid colloquial expressions (e.g. *wicked, gross, telly*).

c. Spelling – your child should be able, most of the time, to:

- Spell correctly any phonetically regular syllable (e.g. ful, plex, org, lect).
- Spell correctly words and syllables with consonant blends and clusters (e.g. *pledge, think, stretch*).
- Demonstrate an understanding of how to spell long vowel sounds even though he may mistakenly choose the wrong spelling (e.g. *dreem* for *dream* shows an understanding, whereas *drem* does not).
- Spell correctly all of the sight words on the list of the 220 most commonly-used words (see Appendix A).
- Spell the words for his age or year group, as found in published spelling lists (see Appendix B).
- Spell correctly (including correct punctuation and use of capital letters) the following information:
  - full name
  - full address and telephone number
  - full names of all family members
  - names of teachers
  - name and address of school
  - birth date
  - friends' names.
- Spell correctly the words for:
  - days of the week, months
  - seasons
  - colours
  - shapes

- mathematical terms
- familiar animals
- holidays
- favourite sports, hobbies, activities, etc.
- common foods.

- Be willing to make a sensible guess as to the spelling of an unfamiliar word, rather than deciding to write an easier word instead.
- Put words in alphabetical order.
- Use a dictionary (see Appendix B).

d. Punctuation – your child should:

- Put a full stop, question mark or exclamation point at the end of every sentence.
- Use apostrophes for contraction (e.g. *isn't*) and possession (e.g. *the boy's house*) but not for plurals.
- Use commas to separate items in a list.

e. Capital letters – your child should:

- Begin all sentences with capital letters.
- Not use capital letters in the middle of words (particular offenders: S, L, K, B).
- Understand the concepts of common nouns and proper nouns as an aid to remembering which words to capitalise.

f. Handwriting – your child should:

- Keep the size of his letters even: make capital letters, tall letters and numerals almost touching the top line, and make small letters less than half that size.
- Keep all letters on the line.
- Form letters and numbers correctly, e.g.
    - make *e* open
    - make *a, i, g,* closed
    - cross t neatly.

g. Presentation – your child should:

- Rub out all mistakes thoroughly.
- When writing in pen, neatly cross out any mistakes with one line.
- Follow each teacher's guidelines for underlining, margins, when to skip lines, long or short form of date, etc.

Numeracy

1. Mental arithmetic

a. Memorisation

These and similar skills should be automatic and almost instantaneous:

- Recognise instantly, without having to count, groups of objects in patterns (e.g. ooo is 3; ooo oo is 5).
- Count to 1,000 by 1, 2, 5, 10, 100.
- Add and subtract from any number, e.g.:
    - plus one, plus two, plus three (by first adding two and then adding one)
    - minus one, minus two, minus three (by first subtracting two and then subtracting one)
    - plus ten or any multiple of ten.
- Know the number combinations (addition and subtraction) up to 20, so that counting on fingers or making little marks on the paper is unnecessary. Examples:

    $7 + 3 = 10$
    $9 - 4 = 5$
    $13 + 4 = 17$

- Subtract mentally by counting on from the smaller number to the larger number.
- Read long numbers correctly by putting the commas in the correct places.
- Instantly know the multiplication and division facts up to 10×10
    - in isolation, not just in sequence.
    - when phrased in different ways, e.g.
        - What times 4 makes 36?

- How many 3's are there in 24?
- What times what equals 30?

b. Understand, remember, and use strategies and short-cuts for calculation, e.g.:

- Add 9 to a number by first adding 10 and then subtracting 1.
- Multiply a number by 10 by putting a nought at the end of the number.

c. Understand basic concepts of

- time
- measurement
- money
- months
- shapes
- place value, etc.

(See Appendix B for helpful guides.)

d. Mathematical terminology

Recognise, use correctly and explain or define mathematical words, e.g.:

decrease	half	remainder
difference	hour	save
double	increase	second
dozen	midday	share
equals	minus	sign
estimate	minute	total
even and odd numbers	plus	twice
fortnight	product	worth
fraction	quarter	

(See Appendix B for publications that clarify these and other mathematical terms.)

e. Understand and solve word problems

- Listen to a simple sum or word problem and perform the calculations mentally.

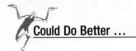

- Correctly complete all of the sums and problems expected of his age or year group, as found in published workbooks (see Appendix B).

2. Written arithmetic

Your child should understand and remember how to do the following, with increasing accuracy, speed and neatness:

- write numbers to 1,000 in figures and in words
- addition with carrying
- subtraction with borrowing
- short multiplication with carrying
- short division with remainder
- translate simple word problems into "number sentences" and solve.

General knowledge

For example, your child should be able to recall and explain clearly:

- the full names of family members, their birthdays, schools, occupations, etc.
- today's date
- the months of the year in order
- the seasons in order
- which months are in which seasons
- the days of the week in order
- some basic facts and concepts about the following topics:

animals	the human body
current events	nutrition
famous people	occupations
geography	plant life
history	weather
holidays	

Mature habits

Without certain habits, a child cannot fulfil his potential or be successful at school, no matter how bright he may be:

1 Acting considerately and politely, which includes:
    - making eye contact
    - keeping a polite tone of voice, even when frustrated or upset
    - not laughing at others' mistakes
    - helping others.
2 Following most instructions immediately – without arguing, complaining or asking for exceptions.
3 Remembering and following the school rules and routines, needing very few prompts.
4 Staying on task.
5 Paying attention to all the details of a task (whether the task is listening, reading, writing, drawing, debating, throwing a ball, feeding the guinea pig, etc.). Paying attention to details is a more precise way of describing what we often call:
    - "doing one's best"
    - "making an effort"
    - "applying oneself"
    - "using common sense".

To be more specific, your child should be learning to do the following without being reminded:

- Wait patiently, listen to instructions and not begin a task until told to begin.
- Understand and act on a series of 3-4 instructions, without needing repetition.
- Use common sense to solve problems, rather than asking unnecessary questions.
- Work in silence (for 5 minutes at a time when he enters reception, gradually increasing to 15-30 minutes by entry to secondary school).
- Work in a small team with classmates, sharing equipment and ideas.

- Always take a sensible guess, rather than leaving any blanks.
- Bring his focus back to his work even when there are distractions.
- Not copy anyone else's work.
- Proof-read his work and make corrections.
- Stop an activity as soon as instructed to
- Manage without going to the toilet for one hour.
- Bring a fully equipped pencil case to school and take responsibility for all his possessions.

A few children in each class are naturally "good at" the five classroom habits from an early age. The majority of the class, however, will need lots of encouragement and guidance from their teachers to gradually develop these important habits. And a few children do not seem to improve much in these five habits, despite their teachers' best efforts, year after year. Sometimes these children are simply immature, and will catch up with their peers in a few years, without needing any intervention. But often these worrying gaps in willingness, social awareness, concentration, memory and attention to detail are caused by subtle specific learning difficulties. See Section II for an in-depth discussion of how these difficulties affect all aspects of the child's life at school and at home.

Pupils with subtle specific learning difficulties have unexplained patches of academic under-achievement. In some subjects and with some tasks they struggle more than we would expect, given their level of intelligence and how well they are able to function in other areas.

These are also often the pupils who fidget, fiddle, whisper to their neighbours when everyone else is reading silently, interrupt the lesson to ask an irrelevant question, take ages to settle into an activity and then produce very little, and don't seem to hear the teacher's instruction until it has been repeated several times.

It often seems as if their difficulties with understanding and remembering are caused by an unwillingness to pay attention or "take school seriously." Teachers, being human, become increasingly irritated when the smooth flow of the lesson is interrupted, yet again, by the child who appears as if he can't be bothered to pay attention. Teachers can find it very frustrating trying to teach, contain and motivate these children.

Because learning and attention difficulties often lead to behaviour problems, when parents discover how to help a child improve in academic areas, improvements are often noticed in behaviour and attention as well. Children with subtle specific learning difficulties *can* learn the five important habits necessary for school success, but they will not pick them up just by observing their classmates. Nor will they simply grow out of their annoying, counter-productive ways. And they will certainly not improve through being reprimanded, shouted at or punished.

One important way that parents can help children to achieve their potential is to choose to see the school as a partner, not as an adversary. The following recomendations will help.

Communicating effectively with your child's school

A Put time and thought into building a positive relationship with your child's teachers long before any problems arise. This will smooth the way when you do need to address an uncomfortable situation. There are several ways to establish rapport with teachers, and I suggest you do them all:

> 1 Whenever you see any of the teachers, even in passing, smile and greet them by name. This has the added benefit of influencing your child to like, trust and respect his teachers more.
>
> 2 *Frequently* notice and mention any aspects of the teaching or of the school's ethos that you are pleased about. If you cannot do this in person, you can send notes in to school every week. (When parents are angry and are feeling powerless to affect how the school is dealing with their child, they may not feel able to focus on the positive. But the positive can always be found, if we make a decision to look for it.)
>
> 3 Attend as many school events as possible, not only the twice-yearly parents' evenings but also the special evenings explaining

aspects of the curriculum, the parents' association meetings and fundraisers such as jumble sales and fetes, etc. Think of it as an investment in your child's community.

4 Mark all relevant events on the calendar so that you do not forget or double-book. Use a large family calendar that hangs at your child's eye level and write these events in neatly so that your child can easily read them. He will see how seriously you take his education.

5 Help in the classroom or around the school, volunteer to accompany school outings, help with fundraising, or become a school governor. Even a working parent with a heavy schedule can usually arrange to spare one hour each fortnight to contribute to the school community. Not only will you learn a lot about the school, but you will be in a good position to influence practices and policies.

6 Make a point of learning as much as you can, on an ongoing basis, about

- the teachers: their names, their strengths and weaknesses, how they view the class, how they view your child
- the curriculum
- how progress is monitored
- methods of teaching
- methods of behaviour management, including rules and consequences
- how teachers want homework to be dealt with at home

B Meetings with teachers to discuss a problem:

1 If something is bothering you, don't wait for the next parents' evening, which may be weeks or months in the future.

2 Do not approach the teacher right before or right after school with, "Can I have a quick word?" or "How was he today?" Even if the teacher is able to spare a few minutes, discussing your child within his hearing may embarrass him. If his peers overhear the exchange, it can influence how they see him, and it can solidify a problematic reputation. Most important of all, effective problem-

solving requires more than a few rushed minutes. Instead, make an appointment to meet, not just with your child's teacher, but also with the head teacher, or at least with the head of year. This step registers how seriously you are taking the issue, and it spreads the responsibility for solutions upwards.

3 Whenever possible, both parents should attend every meeting with teachers. This display of United Front will impress both the school and your child.

4 Single parents can bring a friend for support and to take notes.

5 Prepare yourself for the meeting by making thorough notes of

- all your questions and concerns
- what you think might work to solve or alleviate the problem.

Practise phrasing complaints as requests.

6 If you are feeling anxious or defensive about the upcoming meeting, there are a number of points to remember:

- Smile! It will help you feel better.
- Memories of your own school days can colour and distort your present-day perceptions of the child's school.
- The purpose of the meeting is to start solving a problem, not to apportion blame.
- Finding and implementing solutions is the responsibility of all concerned, including the pupil.
- Teachers are human and will become and sound irritable when faced with persistent problems (just as parents do).
- The staff want to help your child, but they are also concerned with the needs of the other pupils (but they are not allowed to discuss these with you).
- Your views about your child and his needs are as important as the teacher's views.
- Many teachers are not sufficiently trained in the area of specific learning difficulties, so you may know more than they do about the causes of your child's problems and the possible solutions.

- You and the staff can work together as a team, but it will not necessarily be an easy partnership.

7 It is best to be honest:

- Acknowledge if you are having similar kinds of problems with your child at home, so that a true picture can emerge.
- For the same reason, share all reports and assessments with the school, including a summary of the findings. (Check after two weeks to find out whether all of your child's teachers have received and read the summary and whether they feel willing and able to put the assessors' suggestions into practice in their classroom.)
- If you are following all or some of the "School Success Skills" recommendations, explain this to the staff. Whatever you have tried, let the school know how long you tried it for and how successful it was.
- State clearly but non-aggressively whenever you agree or disagree.

8 Keep asking questions until you thoroughly understand what the school thinks and what they will do.

"Can you give me an example of..."
"Could you explain it to me again?"
"Why do you think this is happening?"
"What changes can you make to meet my child's needs?"
"When will you do that?"
"Is there a written policy about that?"
"What will happen next year?"
"What is the mentor's name and background?"

9 Take notes during the meeting so that you do not have to rely on your memory, which may well be swamped with lots of information and strong emotions. Write down who will do what and arrange for the school to receive a copy, so that all parties are absolutely clear about what has been agreed.

10 Before the meeting ends, make a date for the next meeting. If this is an ongoing problem, have frequent meetings, at least fortnightly, to support everyone to fulfil their agreements and to monitor how the child is responding. In between the meetings, keep a school-home diary that the child, the teachers and the parents all sign every day. This will keep everyone aware of progress or lack of progress.

SECTION II: What happens when children are not fulfilling their potential

Chapter 4

Problems with schoolwork and homework

Learning ability is determined by innate factors and environmental conditions. In this chapter I will explore the ways in which a child's individual learning style can cause problems in the classroom and with homework. When we talk about learning style we are referring to a particular child's unique combination of learning strengths and learning weaknesses.

In any mainstream classroom there will be marked differences in ability, although most children will fall roughly within the normal range. Some children can focus for a long time, even on difficult material, while others are more distractible and impulsive. Some will understand and enjoy mathematics or the sciences but struggle with literacy. Some pupils will remember a fact or concept or procedure after being told it once or twice, whereas other pupils need many, many repetitions.

It is tempting, but too simplistic, to conclude that the quick learners are the more intelligent pupils and will, of course, do well, while the slower learners are less intelligent, and therefore bound to do poorly.

Intelligence is usually defined as the ability to acquire and use knowledge and skills. To determine a person's I.Q. (Intelligence Quotient), numerous tests are given. Each test measures a slightly different cognitive (i.e. brain) function. If most of a person's scores are average we say he has average intelligence. If most of his scores are high, we say that he is highly intelligent. And if most of his scores are low, we would say he is less intelligent.

But a significant minority of people (estimates range from approximately one-tenth to one-third of the population) do not fall into such neat categories. Instead they have some high scores, some low scores and some

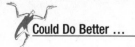

average scores. This is known amongst educational professionals as a "spiky" learning style, and pupils in this category are often called "atypical" learners.

What can we say about the learning ability of these atypical learners? If we were simply to take all their uneven scores and average them out together, we might end up with a number for their I.Q. that was more or less average. But that number would mask a complex situation. This child has some real cognitive strengths, which means that there will be areas where he can learn well and possibly even shine. But he also has some cognitive weaknesses; in some areas he will struggle far more than we would expect.

We would assume, logically, that a child with only mildly spiky scores (particularly if the lows are not very low) or with only a few low scores (and the rest average or high) would experience only slight problems in the classroom. Unfortunately, this child often suffers enormously, both academically and emotionally. There are several reasons for this.

Each part of the brain affects many of our actions. So a child who has even mild impairments in just one or two cognitive functions will have difficulties with many seemingly unrelated learning tasks. Problems with academics, behaviour, attention and social skills often co-exist in the same child because all those issues are affected by the child's learning style. This child, perceiving that he is clearly as intelligent as his peers, is frustrated, confused and embarrassed when his learning does not come easily. To avoid the discomfort of repeatedly disappointing himself or his parents, he may develop resistance tactics, such as time-wasting, negative attention-seeking, misbehaviour or simply fading into the background, saying and doing very little. The more he avoids learning, the further behind he falls, and the more discouraged, and possibly angry, he becomes.

Because this child may be doing well in some aspects of his schoolwork, his parents and teachers are often not aware that he is having genuine difficulties in other areas. They assume that he is just not bothering to try hard enough. He may be labelled lazy, immature or irresponsible. The adults may attempt, through criticism and lecturing and punishments, to encourage him to shoulder his responsibilities. These misguided attempts generally backfire, causing the child to be even more turned off to learning, more anxious and angry, less willing to listen to adults, more prone to misbehave.

In many classrooms there is increasing attention paid by teachers to differentiating the work in order to take into account individual learning differences. But where this does not happen successfully, one result is that some children come to feel like failures, so they gradually switch off more and more. They may talk as if they don't care that they are not doing well, but they often show their true feelings through their behaviour, or rather their misbehaviour. It is easy to look at a child who is being disruptive or who is often off-task and assume that the cause of his problems is his misbehaviour or poor attitude. We think, "If only he would knuckle down and work properly, then he would learn!" But the misbehaviour and the "can't be bothered" attitude are often symptoms of subtle but very real specific learning difficulties.

If some of the child's cognitive scores are extremely low, his difficulties with learning will very soon become evident. Hopefully, he will eventually receive extra help, which may or may not address the real problems. Nowadays he will probably also be given a diagnosis of a "specific learning difficulty" or a "neuro-developmental disorder". Such a diagnosis attempts to explain what is not working well within the brain and which functions are particularly impaired. More terms for disorders are being coined every year, as scientists learn more about how the brain works. Typical diagnoses for children with school problems include:

- Dyslexia
- Dyspraxia
- Attention Deficit Disorder, with or without Hyperactivity
- Disorder of Attention, Motor skills and Perception (DAMP)
- Semantic-Pragmatic Language Disorder
- Communication Disorder
- Non-verbal Learning Disability
- Higher-level Language Disorder
- Sensory Integration Disorder

- Asperger Syndrome
- Autistic Spectrum Disorder
- Obsessive-Compulsive Disorder
- Pathological Demand Avoidance Syndrome

Many children who are diagnosed with one of these disorders are sooner or later also diagnosed, by other professionals, with other disorders from this list. That is because each label describes a different piece of the same puzzle. Each professional naturally focuses on his particular area of expertise, and so will assess and measure a different aspect of the same cognitive impairment.

Pupils exhibiting persistent problems with attention, learning, behaviour or social skills can benefit from testing, initially by an educational psychologist, to confirm or rule out specific learning difficulties and to determine their learning style and cognitive abilities.

What often happens is that a child who is having real problems in the classroom or with homework is diagnosed by professionals as having only a mild specific learning difficulty. Parents are confused and disheartened: why does a mild cognitive impairment cause so many problems? And what can the parents do to rectify the problem?

Often the missing piece of the puzzle has to do with the child's habits. A problem that starts out as mild can become more and more serious or severe over time, if the child is allowed to drift into the unproductive, confidence-sapping habit of avoidance.

Increasingly, due to recent government initiatives, pupils with these and other diagnoses are being expected to cope in a mainstream classroom with very little specialist instruction. And mainstream teachers are being expected, often with little or no targeted training, to somehow know how to handle these learning difficulties and the secondary behavioural problems which they spawn. The result is often frustrated pupils and frustrated teachers.

The human brain is a highly malleable organ. With sufficient repetition, new neural pathways can be laid down and deepened. So children with specific learning difficulties *can* increase the accuracy and speed with which their brain functions. But the improvements will not come from our lecturing, criticising, becoming impatient or just by giving them extra practice. Any adult response that feels to the child as if he is being blamed will make him even less willing to put in the extra effort required. Extra practice can be useful but only if it consists of very frequent and closely-supervised practice of very tiny, do-able "micro-skills." Micro-skills are the very small skills that make up larger skills.

By guaranteeing that most of the child's efforts will result in success, this type of frequent, structured practice strengthens the neural pathways a bit more each time. And success breeds success. The child becomes more confident, more enthusiastic, more willing to put in the extra effort needed. Without the right kind of training, the problems will remain, year after year, despite lots of extra practice.

In order to solve a problem, we must see the problem clearly. The term 'processing' refers to what the brain does with all the information that comes into it through our senses. We need to understand that cognitive processing impairments can adversely affect academic achievement at any of the five stages of learning:

1 Input
2 Integration
3 Memory storage
4 Memory retrieval
5 Output and transfer

Teachers and parents tend to focus most of their concern on the last stage, Output, which is the most visible and seems the most important. It is not always easy to recognise or remember that Output problems are merely symptoms, usually caused by earlier cognitive difficulties at the stages of input, integration, memory storage or memory retrieval.

Processing problems show up in numerous ways, some of which look like misbehaviour or disrespect. To complicate matters further, children with specific learning difficulties often have a particular cluster of temperament characteristics that also tend to make learning and focusing more problematic (see Chapter 5).

1. Input problems

Information enters the brain through our five senses. For academic learning, the auditory and the visual channels are the most important. Learning difficulties may be the result of problems with how the brain records (perceives) the information. These input problems are in the areas of:

    a Discrimination
    b Figure-ground recognition
    c Speed

Most people have brains that are far more efficient at processing visual information, as compared to the processing of auditory information. This is especially true of most children with specific learning difficulties, whose auditory processing is often subtly but significantly impaired.

Auditory perception

"Receptive language" is the term professionals use for our understanding of the language we hear. Weaknesses in this cognitive function contribute to many problems with learning and with social interactions. Spoken language, reading aloud, spelling and peer relationships can all be affected.

A. Discrimination

The child may have difficulty distinguishing the subtle differences between similar sounds. This will lead him to misunderstand what the speaker has said and to respond incorrectly. He may not easily be able to hear the difference between *blue* and *blow* or *poor* and *Paul*. When greeted with "How are you?" he may reply "I'm ten" because he has misheard the *are* for *old*.

This problem, like all the cognitive weaknesses I will describe, is a difficulty but it is not a total inability. With effort, concentration, a bit more time allowed for processing the incoming information and with targeted practice, this child's brain *can* learn to hear these subtle differences more accurately.

Because parents and teachers realise that effort and concentration can produce improvement, they may assume that the child's main problem is one of inattention or "laziness". But we need to remember that most children do not need to be paying particular attention in order for their brains to be able to hear these differences. The majority of children have brains that know how to process the information automatically and efficiently, without any conscious effort being necessary. Any brain that has to keep making such a big effort, just to accomplish what the other brains in the classroom can do without thinking about it, will soon become exhausted. The child with auditory processing problems may also become emotionally exhausted and disenchanted with the whole idea of school and learning.

B. Figure–ground recognition

From the huge amount of incoming auditory stimuli (this is called the background or "ground"), our brains need to be able to choose which ones to pay attention to (this is called the "figure"). The brain of a child with auditory figure-ground recognition difficulties does not easily or quickly realise what he should be listening to. Even when he is motivated to pay attention, his brain finds it difficult to separate out the teacher's voice from the low-level hubbub of rustling papers, pupils whispering in the back row, a door slamming somewhere down the corridor or the noisy radiator. This child seems not to be paying attention in class. But in fact his brain is paying attention to *all* the auditory stimuli and cannot quickly sift through it and choose the most important "noise" to give his undivided attention to. Even after he does tune into what the teacher is saying, he does not easily recognise which are the most important words to think about and remember.

C. Speed

The child may not be able to make sense of what he hears as quickly as necessary. The usual way that our brains make sense of what we hear is by forming a mental picture of it. This is known as "visualising", and it enables us to think about whatever has just been said.

When the teacher is speaking at a normal pace, this child's brain does not turn the words into a mental picture fast enough to keep up, so his brain misses part of the message. He may be struggling to visualise the

first sentence that he hears, or maybe even the first few words of the first sentence. As his brain is laboriously converting the first words he hears into mental images, he misses the next piece of information. He will find the continuing flood of undigested words confusing, frustrating, discouraging or "boring". He may react by tuning out and occupying himself with something more interesting: whispering to a classmate, playing with a toy from his pocket or balancing his ruler on his rubber. Or he may desperately try to keep up, which leads him to interrupt, impulsively blurting out questions which make his classmates groan because the teacher just finished explaining all about that very point.

After many instances of not quite understanding what is said to him, the child comes to believe that there is not much point in listening because it won't make a lot of sense. So without even realising it, he switches off and his attention drifts to something he *can* understand, usually a visual stimulus. He does not know, of course, that he is not listening carefully. Because listening and understanding are internal activities, not visible to an observer, he cannot see that his classmates are paying attention and he is not. He has no way of explaining to himself why they are coping and he is not, so he may conclude that he is stupid.

Because he does not expect to get much useful information or guidance from listening to instructions, he is impatient to begin the activity, before the teacher (or parent) has even finished explaining. This, of course, leads to mistakes. This child needs to be *shown* how to do something, while he is being told.

Because his auditory reaction time is slow, it takes him a few seconds longer to register what he hears, as compared to others of a similar age and similar intelligence. He may develop the habit of automatically responding with "What?" or "Huh?" when spoken to, especially when he is asked a question. Often parents or teachers will then repeat their question or instruction. But if you do not repeat what you said, if instead you stay silent, you will find that often he *has* heard, and he *will* answer you, after a delay of a few seconds.

The child with weak receptive language may adopt the strategy of watching the adult's face, trying to guess from the facial expression if the information is important enough to really try to pay attention to. This habit distracts him from focusing on his task.

One result of poor receptive language is that the child's thinking tends to remain relatively concrete, literal and immature. This is because abstract thought is largely built on an understanding of subtle differences in word meanings.

This child may fidget inordinately or feel "bored" whenever he has to listen without moving for more than a few minutes at a time. However, because this child is usually a strong visual learner, he is easily able to pay attention for hours to visual stimuli, such as video games.

Visual perception

Visual perception describes how the brain takes in and makes sense of what the eyes see. Once again, problems can arise with discrimination, figure-ground recognition and speed of processing.

A. Discrimination

This child's spatial awareness may be confused. This means that he will not easily notice or remember subtle differences in where things are. This can result in some or all of the following problems:

- He may have to consciously think about which is left and which is right each time he needs this information, rather than automatically knowing it.
- He may put his clothes on back to front, calling forth jeers or odd glances from his classmates.
- He may transpose the letters within a word, mistaking *was* for *saw* or *no* for *on*.
- He may also have difficulty noticing small differences in shape. In reading, writing, copying and spelling he may:
  - reverse letters: eg. d/b/p/q/g.
  - confuse E with 3 or S with 5 or, in mathematics, x with +.
  - mentally rotate a 3 and write it as *m*, or a *u* as an *n*.
- His depth perception may be impaired, resulting in difficulties judging distances accurately. Consequently, he may bump into things, trip, fall off his chair or knock over his cup.

- Visual discrimination problems often also show up in visual-motor tasks, in which the brain has to perceive correctly in order to send the correct message telling the hands what to do:
  - Handwriting
  - Cutting and pasting
  - Drawing
  - Ball skills – throwing, catching, hitting, kicking
  - Completing puzzles
  - Using a fork and knife
  - Using tools.

B. Figure–ground recognition

It can be very difficult for a child with visual processing difficulties to choose what to pay attention to amongst the confusing welter of visual stimuli. For example, he knows, in theory, that he should be looking at the teacher at the front of the room, but his visual attention is also drawn to the posters surrounding him on the walls, the comic book being read surreptitiously by a classmate, the scab on his arm, his friend's new rubber and the picture in his textbook. Visual clutter, for example a desk that has on it items not necessary at this very moment, will make concentration difficult.

When he is supposed to be studying the picture in his textbook, his brain may not, unless specifically guided by the teacher, notice the picture's relevance to what the class has just been discussing. Instead, he may focus on a minor detail that happens to capture his attention. Reading comprehension is not just about reading; it is a highly complex set of thinking skills, all of which are adversely affected by processing problems. Once again, adult criticism will not teach this child's brain how to detect and stay focused on the "figure", while blocking out the "ground". Nor will criticism motivate this child to put in the extra effort necessary to try and keep up with his peers.

However, the right kind of practice will accomplish both of these objectives: teaching the child's brain to function more efficiently and also motivating the child to persevere, even when learning is not easy. As before, the practice needs to be closely supervised, requiring only tiny improvements each time, with resultant success.

C. Speed

Some children can look at a picture or a scene or a word and almost
instantly take it in and understand what it is. Other children have brains
that need to look at each bit separately and then make an effort to put
the bits together into an understandable mental picture. This is a
relatively laborious process, which may take longer to accomplish than
parents and teachers think it should take.

2. Integration problems

This is the second stage of learning. This is when understanding takes
place. In a child with subtle learning difficulties, integration may be
inefficient: it may be inaccurate or slow or both. At the Integration stage
the brain is occupied with:

    a Organisation, including sequencing
    b Abstraction.

A. Organisation

To organise something means to arrange it into some kind of system. In
order to be able to store and then use the information that comes in
through the senses, the brain must first organise it.

Children with poor figure-ground recognition are already at a disadvantage
here because, due to a faulty "filter", too much information has entered the
brain, much of it quite irrelevant to the task at hand. But even without that
problem, the brain still has a massive job of organising to do.

One way that the brain organises information is through association.
New bits of information are linked to previously-learned bits. This
explains why it is that the more one knows about a topic the easier it is to
learn and remember additional information about that topic and also
about related topics. This is also the explanation for a distressing fact of
school life: without effective intervention, as children with subtle specific
learning difficulties grow older, the gap in educational attainment
between them and their peers widens. The more their peers know, the
easier it is for them to learn more. But the weaker a child's academic

skills are, particularly the basics of literacy in its widest sense (listening, understanding, speaking, reading and writing) the more difficult it is for this child to progress. It is as if learning is passing them by.

There is a particular type of organisation that can be especially problematic, and that is *sequential* organisation. Sequencing means putting bits of information into a particular order, which might be

- From lowest value to highest value, e.g. a series of numbers.
- Chronological order, e.g. the days of the week, the months of the year or the seasons.
- From most important to least important, as in an essay.
- An arbitrary but agreed-upon order, such as the letters of the alphabet.

Problems with auditory or visual sequencing show up in many areas:

- Telling a story in a muddled way, e.g. starting in the middle or leaving out important information.
- In speaking, mis-sequencing syllables or letters, e.g. *pasghetti, hopsital, aminals.*
- In mathematics, writing or copying 32 for 23 or carrying the wrong digit in an addition sum.
- In spelling a word, writing all the correct letters, but in the wrong order.

B. Abstraction

Abstraction refers to understanding the meaning of what comes in through the senses. The function of the brain at this stage is to generalise from the specific. The brain notices what is similar about several different experiences and extracts or formulates a general principle or idea.

For example, teachers expect that a child who has learned about the "silent e" in words such as *hope, tape* and *fine* will, without much effort, soon be able to read and write other simple words that end in silent e, for example, *cape, bite* and *rode*. But some children's brains do not automatically generalise. These children can learn to generalise, but it will require more conscious effort, more time, and as before, more closely-supervised practice of tiny steps, so tiny that correct responses are almost assured.

Semantics refers to the meaning of words, and pragmatics refers to the way language is generally used. Children with auditory processing weaknesses often have problems in both of these areas. These will interfere with listening comprehension and reading comprehension.

3. Memory storage problems

The next step in academic learning is *Memory Storage* of auditory and visual material. A child with subtle specific learning difficulties often has more trouble storing auditory information accurately.

All information entering the brain goes first into the short-term memory. This is where we keep information that we can manage to hold onto only while we are attending to it. An example is getting a telephone number from the operator and holding it in our head while we dial the number. If we are interrupted in our task and stop attending to the telephone number for a few seconds, the information is lost to us. Some children suffer from inefficient short-term memory storage. Information seems to evaporate from their short-term memory quickly, even when there is no interruption.

Then there is the long-term memory. Once a piece of information is lodged in the long-term memory, it is available to us just by thinking about it, for example our home address.

Paradoxically, a child may have weak short-term memory storage and strong long-term memory storage but still experience problems with storing information in his long-term memory. This is because the short-term memory is the gateway into the long-term memory. After the same piece of information has been put into the short-term memory a certain number of times (more repetitions will be necessary for some children than for others), it then is automatically stored in the long-term memory. But if, due to an impairment, the information keeps falling out of a child's short-term memory, it is not sticking around in the short-term memory long enough for it to be transferred to the long-term memory. Sometimes what goes wrong is that the information was poorly or incorrectly understood, at the Integration stage, and so it is stored incorrectly or incompletely.

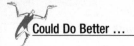

4. Memory retrieval problems

Memory retrieval is the next step in the learning process. Even an efficient retrieval system will not be able to locate information that was never stored or that was stored incorrectly or incompletely. So a child may keep saying "tornado" when he means "volcano", even after he is corrected, because the wrong word was originally stored in his long-term memory. It will take many repetitions *of the right kind* to replace "tornado" with "volcano". Similarly, once a child is in the habit of misspelling a particular word, it is difficult for his brain to remember the correct spelling. He *can* be re-taught, but it will take more than simply telling him, or telling him off, each time he gets it wrong.

In addition, some children have distinct memory retrieval problems. One type is called *dysnomia*, which refers to the annoying tip-of-the-tongue experience which happens to all of us occasionally. We know what we want to say, but we just can't think of the right word. Some children have this experience almost every time they open their mouths, particularly when they are anxious about getting it wrong. They find themselves starting sentences or phrases that they cannot finish, so they backtrack and start afresh. This results in awkward speech, called "dysfluency". They may even say very familiar phrases incorrectly.

Another memory retrieval problem shared by many atypical learners is *fixation*. It is as if the brain gets stuck and keeps coming up with the same response. This child may write down the same answer for several different maths sums. Or he may do very careful addition, even when the sign clearly tells him to subtract, because the last few sums he did were all addition sums. Sometimes a child will see his mistake and conscientiously rub it out, only to write down exactly the same wrong answer all over again.

Working memory refers to the brain's ability to pay attention to several pieces of information at the same time. Many academic tasks require the pupil to be able to do this, e.g. listening to and following instructions at the same time, reading and making notes, remembering the steps needed for a long multiplication sum, copying from the board, proof-reading, etc. When a child's memory does not easily hold several pieces of information, he will find many tasks far more difficult than other children will.

In summary, we can see that every task, every bit of knowledge, every skill and procedure will be affected by problems with memory retrieval.

5. Output and transfer problems

At this stage the child does something with his knowledge. At school, he usually needs to show his teachers that he has learnt something. In most schools, children communicate about what they have learned largely through language, spoken and written. In some subjects pupils will also be expected to physically demonstrate that they have mastered a practical skill.

A child's brain needs to be able to take the general principles he has learned and apply them to new situations. *Transfer* is happening when the brain takes information that has been learned in one form and uses it in a slightly different form.

A. Spoken language

Spoken language can be divided into two separate types: spontaneous and demanded.

A. *Spontaneous language* is initiated by the speaker. He can, in theory, organise his thoughts and search for the right words before he starts to speak. An impulsive child often does not take the time to do this.

A child with dysnomia often develops strategies designed to mask the problem or to buy himself a bit more time to think of the word he is searching for.

- His speech may be peppered with verbal fillers, such as *um, uh, you know, kind of, like, thingy* and *whats-it.*
- He may wave his hands about to help him describe something, or he may offer to draw a picture in explanation.
- He may talk very fast, to get the uncomfortable experience over with quickly.
- He may say "I don't know" or shrug, rather than put himself through the emotionally painful experience of feeling stupid.

Listening to this child is not easy. Putting in the effort to make sense of the language of a dysnomic, dysfluent child can be exhausting. Teachers and parents try to be patient but may become exasperated. Peers are less patient and less forgiving. They may make fun of the child who cannot express himself clearly, or they may simply ignore him, unconsciously excluding him from their games and conversations. Parents often unwittingly perpetuate the problems of dysfluency and immature language. Parents are of course familiar with the child's quirks of expression and usually can understand what he is trying to communicate. They tend to respond to the child as if what he said really makes sense. When someone asks a question of the child, the parents may answer for him or translate his response.

Sometimes parents are well aware of their child's immature or disordered language, but at a loss as to what to do about it. They often worry that pointing out his errors will make an anxious or angry child feel even worse. So they may correct him only occasionally or half-heartedly. Eventually patience runs out and frustration sets in. A stressed parent may explode in irritation or embarrassment, which leaves the child mystified as well as upset.

B. *Demanded Language.* Here the child is responding to a question or instruction. He has no time to plan ahead so he must organise his thoughts and find the right words as he is speaking. When this is difficult for his brain to do, the child may say "What?" or ask for the question to be repeated, even if he has heard it, in an attempt to gain some thinking time. Or he may stare silently back at his questioner, which can look like deliberate defiance. When he speaks he may ramble, talking all around the idea, as often off the point as on it, trying to keep the teacher from asking another question. Or he may babble, hoping that if enough words come out, some of them will be right. Often his brain retrieves the wrong words or incorrect sentence construction, sometimes the wrong concept altogether. He may keep checking the teacher's face anxiously to see if she is satisfied.

Many children with subtle specific learning difficulties are far more comfortable when they are the ones initiating the verbal exchange.

However, an impulsive child who cannot seem to stop talking about whatever grabs his interest may be laughed at by his peers and called "motor-mouth" or "show-off". Adults and peers quickly lose interest in what this child is saying because it is such hard work for the listener, mentally separating the main ideas from the trivial or irrelevant details.

B. Written work

A child with subtle specific learning difficulties is likely to produce a poor standard of written work in comparison with his oral ability. Every aspect of writing is affected by problems at the earlier stages of learning.

1. Length and speed

The child with output difficulties often writes much less than every other pupil in the class, and takes longer to do it. This child may appear to be wasting an inordinate amount of time before he settles down to work. He may sit staring into space while the rest of the class has their heads down, busily writing. He may be thinking about how to capture in words what he wants to convey, or he may be pre-occupied with anxiety. He may use up his writing time by complaining about the task, trying to argue, plead or bargain his way out of it. His usual complaints are that the work is boring or too hard or that his arm or back hurts. And in a way he is right. Trying to pay attention to all the different aspects of writing at the same time is very hard for his brain. And writing may be boring for him because he must focus so much energy on the mechanics of the task, rather than on the more interesting part, which is the content or the creation of a story from his imagination.

2. Content

Due to earlier difficulties at the Input or Integration stages, the child may not quite have understood what he should be writing about. So he may answer at length, but off the point, which is a significant cause of exam failure. He is likely to have difficulties producing ideas (whether from his imagination, from memory or even his opinions), and then organising, developing and expanding his ideas.

3. Choice of language

Even a strong visual learner, one who is good at seeing how things fit together and good at visualising details, may have great difficulty translating his vivid mental images into coherent sentences which do justice to the richness of his imagination. He may end up using a very limited, stilted vocabulary and producing very little.

4. Spelling

Spelling is a spectre which looms large in the mind of a child who does not spell well. Although now most written communication is via computers which automatically check for spelling errors, teachers and parents still give children the impression, unintentionally, that poor spelling is akin to a character defect. Correct spelling is still seen by many as the hallmark not just of an educated person but of a responsible person. The unspoken and unexamined assumption seems to be that the child could spell properly if he would only try harder.

And there is a grain of truth to this belief. It is certainly true that even poor spellers usually can spell much better when they take the time and make the effort to think carefully about spelling. But the effort is more onerous than people generally realise. "Trying harder" uses up so much of the child's attention and takes so much time that it pushes out of the brain many other important aspects of writing, especially creativity, which may also be difficult for this child. And is it fair to expect poor spellers to continually put in this extra effort? Good spellers do not have to "try harder". Their brains happen to be equipped with efficient visual memory storage and retrieval. For these children, correct spelling happens automatically, with very little conscious attention to the matter.

When a child asks how to spell a word, he is often told to "Just try!" or "Sound it out" or "Look it up in the dictionary". For the child with weak visual or auditory processing, these tactics often result in confusion, frustration and the wrong spelling, so understandably he develops a reluctance to try. If he keeps asking how to spell words, parents and teachers will become irritated, often assuming that he simply cannot be bothered to try. So to protect himself from impatience and criticism, he may choose to substitute a simpler word that he definitely knows how to spell instead of his first choice of word, which might well have been more colourful, more accurate, more original or more imaginative. Or he may give up even caring about trying to get the spelling right, opting for a purely phonetic approach or guessing wildly, which can result in bizarre, indecipherable words.

This is most likely to happen if his parents, in a kind-hearted but misguided attempt to make him feel better, assert that they also are no good at spelling. The child can see that his parents are functioning members of the community, able to hold down jobs and care for their family. So he concludes that spelling is something that only teachers care about but that it is not important in "real life".

5. Punctuation and capital letters

Correct usage may continue to be a problem for years, despite reminders and remedial help. Once again, these mistakes may look to parents and teachers like carelessness, laziness or contempt.

6. Handwriting

This is one of the most common output problems. Visual-discrimination and visual-motor difficulties can result in handwriting that is illegible and full of "careless" mistakes, particularly if the child is rushing to get the unpleasant, unsatisfying experience of writing over with as quickly as possible. Occasionally, an anxious or perfectionist child with poor visual-motor processing reacts in the opposite way. Instead of rushing, he evolves the habit of writing very slowly, forming each letter very carefully. This child may produce written work that is a joy to behold. But his concentration on that one aspect of writing has stolen attention away from the other aspects of writing, which will, of course, suffer: content, vocabulary, spelling, punctuation, even accuracy.

7. Presentation and neatness

There are likely to be many crossings out and incompletely rubbed out first attempts, as well as corrections written right over the original

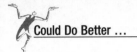

without rubbing out first. Instructions about spacing, margins, underlining etc., are often ignored because the child cannot keep all the relevant information in his working memory.

8. Copying

The act of copying requires the child's brain and eyes to continually shift focus back and forth between two points. This is particularly difficult when what the child is copying from is far away, such as a whiteboard. In addition, his brain may not be adept at holding several words at a time in his short-term memory, so he has to look back at the original after every word he writes, or even after every letter. This is laborious, soul-destroying work, especially for a child with additional handwriting problems. Copying is likely to be very slow, with many inaccuracies creeping in. He may lose his place, resulting in words or whole lines being either omitted or written twice. The focus on accuracy takes up so much of his attention that the child is not even thinking about the meaning of the words he is copying. A pupil once proudly showed me a page of very neat writing about Henry VIII's wives, which she had copied from the blackboard. When I quizzed her about the fates of the wives, she looked at me as if I had asked a very silly question and replied, "I didn't read it! I copied it". If she had had access to a handout, all her mental energy could have been focused on comprehension.

9. Proof-reading

Problems at every earlier stage of learning will affect the child's ability to proof-read accurately. In addition, proof-reading requires a mature willingness to face one's mistakes. So it is not surprising that proof-reading is an area of huge difficulty for most atypical learners.

CHAPTER 5
Behaviour problems at home and at school

All children, simply because they are children, will misbehave at home and at school from time to time. When this happens occasionally, it is nothing to be concerned about (although appropriate sanctions should still be enforced, rather than simply ignoring or telling off).

Of course parents and teachers will be concerned whenever a child's misbehaviour is very problematic, for example deliberately provocative, aggressive or defiant. In addition, there are a host of minor misbehaviours which can also result in major problems and adversely affect school success.

Children who are not doing well at school often have certain behavioural problems in common. These behaviours may on occasion be deliberate, but usually they are impulsive, compulsive or habitual. Each of these behaviours, when viewed on its own, may seem quite mild and harmless. But these behaviours usually come in clusters, and they can cause severe suffering and anguish for the children and for their parents, siblings, teachers and classmates.

These behaviours, which I outline below, keep the child from fulfilling his academic potential and draw negative comments from adults and peers. The child experiences ongoing frustration, embarrassment, anger and erosion of confidence. He may get caught in a downward spiral of lower and lower self-esteem, less and less trust in and respect for his parents and teachers and more and more problematic behaviours.

Teachers and the child's classmates suffer when the peace and quiet necessary for learning is continually disrupted. Dealing with these minor but frequent misbehaviours absorbs a great deal of the teacher's time and patience, with not much left over for the other pupils.

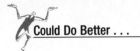

Some of these typical misbehaviours are called primary problems because they are the direct result of the specific learning difficulties I discussed in Chapter 4 or of an inborn temperament which is extremely sensitive, intense, impulsive and emotionally immature. Other common behaviours are considered secondary problems because they stem from the unintentional mismanagement, at home and at school, of the learning difficulties or the extreme temperament. Primary behaviours are caused by "nature", and secondary behaviours are caused by "nurture". Both the primary and the secondary problems can be mild or severe.

Primary behaviour problems are noticeable very early in a child's life, often long before he first goes to school. It is assumed, often mistakenly, that these behaviours are caused simply by immaturity and that with time the child will naturally grow out of them and into more mature, more sensible behaviour. Certainly, children mature over time, but because the tendency towards these primary behaviour problems is hard-wired in the child's brain, he will not simply outgrow them. He can, however, be taught and trained in more mature habits, responses and attitudes.

Many children are relatively more focused and co-operative at school, as compared to at home. This is because the tighter structure of the school day helps train them in the habit of following routines and rules. Even so, primary behaviour problems are apparent both at home and at school:

1. Poor sustained concentration, attention or effort

This is often called inattentiveness, distractibility or short attention span. This child often:

- Is distracted by sights and sounds around him.
- Is not listening to the adult when he should be.
- Does not readily follow instructions.
- Fails to finish routine tasks unless closely supervised.
- Jumps from one uncompleted activity to another.
- Ignores or becomes impatient with details because he feels he has understood the general idea: "I get it".
- Is quickly "bored" (especially if the task or activity is repetitive, time-consuming, unsupervised or not of his own choosing).

- Has great difficulty getting started on "boring" tasks.
- Has very poor attention to detail during "boring" tasks.
- Seems to become physically tired and lethargic when faced with "boring" tasks.
- May seem "spacey" and unfocused.
- Has great difficulty getting and staying organised.
- Does not remember what other children his age easily remember.
- Chatters off the subject.
- Wants to be entertained; he rarely plays by himself.

2. Weak impulse control for delay of gratification

This child often:

- Starts working before getting the directions clear or before listening to all of the directions.
- Does not seem to remember often-repeated rules or routines, although his impulse control is (relatively) better one-on-one or with a respected authority figure.
- Acts or speaks before stopping to think about the consequences
- Resists correcting his work or says (and believes) that he has when he has merely glanced at it.
- Does not readily learn from his mistakes or from the consequences of his actions, so continues to make inappropriate or unwise decisions.
- Interrupts, blurts out, asks unnecessary questions, talks excessively, does not seem to notice that no one is listening, is tactless, disruptive.
- Makes noise during quiet activities.
- Makes jokes in the middle of a serious, or even a sad, conversation
- Does not seem to notice or care about what the rest of the class is doing: lacks deference or a sense of occasion (this can be mistaken for confidence or showing off).
- Grabs, does not wait his turn, does not want to share.
- Shifts excessively from one activity to another.

- Is drawn to activities that are immediately rewarding; opts for smaller, quicker rewards rather than working towards larger, long-term rewards.
- Looks for black-and-white answers, solutions that seem simple or easy.
- When faced with a problem, will become "bored" or find some external reason not to continue looking for a solution.
- When faced with uncertainty (for example with choices where there is not just one obviously correct response) will quickly make a decision, without thinking it through; later he will often want to change his choice.
- Does not consider, or even notice, others' needs or feelings
- Is unreceptive to the opinions of others, unwilling to consider alternative points of view so has difficulty modifying his thinking or behaviour based on what others say.
- Blames others when things do not go as he wants or expects
- May lash out verbally or physically; he is quick to anger and prone to unpredictable aggressive reactions.
- Rushes into potentially dangerous situations.

3. Excessive task-irrelevant activity or movement

This child:

- is very fidgety, restless, "on the go"
- is often not sitting *still*, even when he is sitting; some part of his body is almost always in motion: wriggling, tapping, rocking, shifting position, doodling, humming, fiddling with any object within reach
- has great difficulty sitting still when doing "boring" tasks
- finds a reason to be out of his seat
- runs instead of walks
- seems driven to interact with peers and siblings, even when this clearly annoys them
- when not in front of a screen, wants to be *doing* something; parents say he rarely settles down or relaxes.

4. Sensitive temperament, both physically and emotionally, with intense reactions:

This child is often *physically* very sensitive; he may well have one or more of the following:

- hyper-acute senses, being inordinately bothered by bright lights, loud noises and certain smells, tastes and textures
- sleep disturbances – he may have difficulty getting to sleep or be prone to nightmares, night terrors, sleep-walking or talking in his sleep
- skin problems, which can be mild (dry, itchy skin) or severe (eczema)
- allergies or food intolerances
- digestive problems – constipation or diarrhoea, sometimes both
- respiratory infections and ear, nose and throat problems, which can range from recurring colds and "glue ear" to hay fever and asthma.

Due to the physical problems, this child is often not feeling one hundred percent. As a result, he may be irritable or inclined to tears and sulks. This child is also *emotionally* very sensitive; he easily feels:

- frustrated
- over-excited
- impatient, annoyed
- enthusiastic, exuberant
- competitive
- angry
- envious, jealous
- anxious about future events
- confused
- unrealistically over-confident or under-confident
- worried, fearful
- aggressive, vengeful
- unsettled, especially by changes, transitions and disruptions to his routine

- hard done by, blaming others, feeling left out, betrayed, victimised, teased, bullied, hurt, misunderstood, unfairly treated; he takes things personally, including small (or even imagined) slights.

5. Ongoing craving for external stimulation:

This child is often drawn to and easily distracted by activities which are new, exciting or high-risk, including rule bending and testing. He resists going back over familiar material because it seems extremely "boring". He is a thrill-seeker, in small or large ways.

6. Perseveration, which is also called:

insatiability	relentlessness	stubbornness
fixation	pre-occupation	obsession
compulsion	hyper-focus	addictive behaviour
narrow interests	restricted interests	chronic inflexibility

Perseveration can take the form of continuing a behaviour automatically and often involuntarily (such as spelling *banana* as *bananana*, rubbing out a mistake until he makes a hole in the paper or repeating a joke or silly noise, even after being told not to). He may have difficulty making the transition from one topic or activity or even from one thought to another. Often it looks as if he is ignoring the teacher's instructions or deliberately refusing to co-operate.

Because of his drive for high stimulation, typical pre-occupations often revolve around activities and topics which include a strong element of danger or aggression, such as weapons, violent computer games or military history. He may develop a fascination for objects or activities that are forbidden (such as crime), restricted (for example, sweets) or usually reserved for adulthood (such as category 18 films).

On the other hand, the fixations may be entirely age-appropriate and harmless. These can still cause problems in several ways. For example, the child may strenuously resist playing with any but a certain few toys or listening to any but a certain few stories. This can significantly limit his exposure to the wealth of other activities available at home and at school.

Often a child with this temperament is inflexible when it comes to familiar routines. He is apt to complain or argue more than other children when life does not go as he wants or expects. He feels that he *needs* to wear the red t-shirt to the park, *needs* to find the exactly right Lego™ piece or else his spaceship will not be any good, *needs* his special stuffed animal tucked up in bed next to him or else he can't sleep.

7. Poor social skills

This child is often not aware of the impact that his behaviour has on others' perceptions of him. For example, he stands too close and talks too loud, even though he has been told many times that this irritates people. When he must greet someone he often mumbles, scowls and avoids eye contact. When he is losing at a game, he calls his playmates names or accuses them of cheating; then he is hurt and mystified when they exclude him from the next game.

8. Unpredictability

He has considerably greater than average variability in his academic performance, with extreme changes from one day to the next, or even within the same day. This unpredictability impacts on many aspects of his school work and homework:

- willingness
- concentration
- comprehension
- memory
- attention to detail: accuracy, thoroughness and presentation
- patience and perseverance
- the amount of work he produces
- speed (he may vacillate between rushing through his work and dawdling).

His behaviour and social skills are also very variable, with sudden mood swings and unexpected episodes of aggression or withdrawal.

Strengths

Atypical learners often share certain strengths as well. Unfortunately, many of these strengths can land an impulsive child in trouble time and time again. Most of the characteristics listed below can be a distinct liability until the child develops a more mature degree of self-control. As the child absorbs and internalises responsible, productive habits, he learns to use his strengths to his advantage. He is then able to contribute to the school community, and his self-confidence soars. The atypical learner often:

- is a creative, lateral thinker
- seems very bright outside of school
- has quick responses (especially for self-chosen activities)
- monitors his surroundings constantly, with excellent attention for novel aspects of the environment
- is capable of extreme focus (mostly for self-chosen activities)
- can be flexible and imaginative, capable of changing strategy quickly (when the goal is of his own choosing)
- has a high energy level
- is a strong visual thinker
- faces danger willingly
- is giving, affectionate and caring
- has a good long-term memory
- is talented (often excelling in art, sports or music)
- has a strong sense of humour.

Academic strengths are often in the areas of science, history, other fact-based subjects, sometimes mathematics, sometimes practical subjects.

At this point you may be wondering what has caused your child to come into the world with this extreme temperament. Usually a child's temperament is part of his unique genetic inheritance. That is why difficulties with attention, learning, behaviour, social skills and allergies tend to run in families, although each family member may exhibit a different piece of the puzzle. One sibling may have reading and writing problems despite being very advanced verbally; another sibling may be extremely impulsive, loud and wild. A cousin may be painfully shy and possibly clumsy, while an uncle, even though very able, may have drifted, through much of his life, from one unrewarding job to the next.

In addition to the genetic inheritance from parents, the primary problems may be compounded by very early environmental factors, such as a difficult pregnancy or birth complications. In rare cases, the cause of the problems may be minimal brain damage, due to disease, trauma or toxins that affect the central nervous system.

Secondary problems

Secondary problems are created by the environment, in particular by how parents and teachers react to the primary problems. As we have seen, it is all too easy to mistake genuine processing problems and the resultant lack of confidence for laziness or disrespect. When parents and teachers do not understand the real causes of under-achievement or misbehaviour, they tend to react negatively: repeating, reminding, reprimanding, blaming, punishing. This negativity further saps the child's motivation to make the effort to learn and to behave.

The secondary problem of chronic low self-esteem is a typical result of primary problems that have not been adequately addressed. This child no longer sees himself accurately. He does not recognise his strengths and abilities, and he also develops a reluctance to acknowledge his weaknesses and mistakes, over-reacting to even mild criticism, suggestions or advice. He may become very susceptible to peer pressure, trying to buy friendship by becoming the class clown or the neighbourhood daredevil.

If the primary problems of subtle specific learning difficulties and extreme temperament are not dealt with effectively, by adolescence the secondary problems can lead to more and more severe academic underachievement and disruptive misbehaviour. This can result in suspensions, exclusion, school refusal and truancy.

The typically immature social skills of atypical learners contribute to their easily developing into bullies or into the victims of bullies. Sometimes this child is both: he may be bullied at school, and he may be a charming tyrant at home.

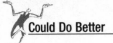

In the most extreme cases, this child may grow into a teenager who becomes involved in substance misuse, irresponsible sexual activity, delinquency and even crime. I know this statement is a strong one, and it may seem unnecessarily alarmist. The important thing to keep in mind is that it is never too late for parents to start reversing such a tendency. How effective you will ultimately be, and how quickly you will start to see results, depends of course on numerous factors:

- the child's age when you begin to effectively address his problems
- the severity or degree of his difficulties
- the strength of your determination to remain positive, firm and consistent, and
- how vigorously you advocate for your child with the school and with other professionals.

At any stage we can embark on a programme to help our children learn how to learn and learn how to control themselves. With some children this will be our toughest but also our most rewarding job.

SECTION III: Establishing enjoyable and productive homework habits

Chapter 6
Clarifying the homework routines and rules

How do we make the routines and rules we believe are right clear to our children? And then how do we make sure that our children actually stick to them? How do we keep ourselves from giving in or turning a blind eye when we are exhausted or in a hurry?

Only a very, very few children have the maturity and motivation to create productive homework routines for themselves with no help from parents. For most children and teenagers, enjoyable, productive homework habits need to start out as rules that parents initially lay down as law. We must not expect our children to be happy about the new rules at first. But if we persevere, staying *friendly and firm*, over time (and sooner than you think possible) resistance fades, and the rules become accepted, and even appreciated, routines. This process of establishing enjoyable and productive homework habits is accomplished in three stages. Briefly, the stages are:

1   Clarifying what you expect from your child and from yourself so that everyone in the family knows exactly what the routines and rules are, and everyone knows that everyone knows. This makes it much harder for children to divide and conquer, e.g. "But Dad said I didn't have to". Clarifying the routines and rules, in and of itself, can prevent many (but not all) flare-ups of misbehaviour. By preparing for success we make it much easier for children to remember and to do the right thing rather than to do the wrong thing.

2   Closely supervising the daily homework sessions, insisting on the homework habits that you have decided are right for your family. (See Chapter 7 for a comprehensive list of useful homework habits.)

3   Following through with rewards and consequences in order to reinforce the homework habits you want or to nip in the bud anything that is starting to go wrong.

These three stages can be used to establish routines and rules for homework and also for bedtimes, mealtimes, household chores, etc. and any other habits that are important to you. The following guidelines will make establishing homework routines and rules much easier:

- Remember that a child's tempo is much slower than an adult's. If we try to get children to do things faster than is comfortable for them, misbehaviour of one sort or another will result. So we need to build some extra time into every part of a child's routine.
- Less is more. There will be times when all the homework won't get done, so go for quality over quantity. Simplify the routines by focusing on the very important tasks.
- You may find that you are not putting rules and routines into place because you are not sure what you can legitimately expect from your child at each age or developmental stage. Rather than allowing the child to decide what he will do, make the time to find out what he can do.

Stage 1, clarifying the homework routines and rules:

A   Parents need to set aside a chunk of time, perhaps half an hour, with no children around and with no other distractions. Together, list all the routines and rules that you want to see happening, even if you cannot quite believe that you could ever make them happen consistently. Where necessary, compromise for a united front. And no criticising of the other partner's ideas! If you are a single parent, do this stage with a friend. Two heads are better than one. Once you know what you want the homework routines and rules to be, write them down.

B   In addition to specific rules for specific situations, have a few over-arching rules that will cover many different situations. I suggest the following all-purpose rules for children:

- Do what you are told, first time, without a fuss. (This covers what you want them to start doing as well as what you want them to stop doing.)
- Instead of interrupting a parent who is talking, say "Excuse me" and then *wait* for the parent to stop talking and to look at you.
- Put things back where they belong.
- Ask, and wait for permission, before you touch someone else's belongings.
- Instead of complaining, make a polite request.

C Now make up and write down some rules and routines *for yourself* to follow. These will improve co-operation much faster than any rules we make for our children! For example, a powerful rule for parents is: As soon as you find that you are getting annoyed with your children, immediately switch into Descriptive Praise mode (see Chapter 8). This will usually gain you co-operation more quickly than any other tactic.

D At a neutral time, *both parents* sit down with *one child* to discuss homework routines. Talking to each child separately enables you to tailor the rules for each. Also, the possibly mocking or obstructive attitude of one child will not influence the other siblings.

- Call them routines rather than rules. This usually makes them more palatable, especially for teenagers.
- Emphasise that this discussion will last no more than ten minutes, and set a timer to make sure that you stop the meeting *exactly* on time. An angry or resistant child will be able to accept and participate in such a discussion more willingly when he knows that the ordeal he anticipates will soon be over. You will need to have additional ten-minute meetings daily until you are satisfied that everyone in the family knows and understands all the homework routines and rules.
  Open the discussion by explaining (in an assertive voice, not in either a tentative or an irritated voice) that parents as well as children have responsibilities about homework. Draw a line down the centre of a blank piece of paper and label the two

sides something like: "Mum and Dad need to," and "Henry needs to". Instead of telling the child what the routines and rules are, ask each person in turn, starting with the child, to say some of the homework responsibilities that he can think of, whether yours or his own. You will be pleasantly surprised to discover that your child knows most of the routines and rules, even those which he regularly ignores or continually tries to negotiate about. Write down neatly in the correct columns any that you agree with, refraining from making any comments that your child could possibly perceive as negative.

E One parent reported that her son initially replied with: "Mum, write down on your side that you should stay out of it. The school says it's our responsibility. We're old enough". This mother bit her tongue and managed not to retort with a snappy one-liner: "I'll be glad to stay out of it when you can prove to me that you're doing it properly". Instead, she took a deep breath to calm herself and said, with a smile, "My job is to help you get into good habits. So I can't stay out of it just yet because you still need help with some of your habits, like starting early enough. But maybe pretty soon I'll be able to. We would both like that". By pausing and collecting her thoughts before she spoke, the mother conveyed the same information, but in a much more positive, less blaming way.

F Eventually the family, working as a team, will have generated and recorded in detail all the homework routines and rules that are consistent with the parents' values.

G To help an impulsive or resistant child to accept the new routines and rules more easily, parents can prepare for success by doing many short "talk-throughs" every day. A talk-through is a technique that increases the likelihood that your child will be co-operative by jogging his memory about what you expect. But a talk-through is not a reminder or a reprimand, neither of which are very effective. A talk-through is quite different. It happens *before* the event, and it is the child, not the adult, who does the talking. The parent asks leading questions and the child explains in detail what he should do and not do. Each talk-through takes only a minute or two and leaves the child with a clearer mental image of himself doing the right thing. Repeated talk-throughs sprinkled throughout the day serve to make this mental image ever more vivid and more real to the child. Soon he is falling in with the new routines, with less and less fuss.

H Use the list of rules that you have generated as an aide-memoir during the daily homework sessions. The list will remind you of the many things that your child is *not* doing wrong at this moment. You will find that there is much more to praise than you initially thought. The more that our children hear about their O.K. behaviour, the more of it we will see.

Clarifying the rules and routines is the essential first step towards establishing sensible homework habits. Clarity encourages parents to notice and mention every tiny step towards compliance with the routines. This is a far more positive way to effect change than nagging when the child does not co-operate.

Being clear about exactly what is expected will eliminate a great deal of resistance. Your child can no longer plead ignorance or confusion. He may still be prone to convenient forgetting, but Stage 3, Following through (see Chapter 8), will drastically reduce forgetting, both real and pretend.

Chapter 7
Useful routines and rules for improving homework habits

School is a child's "job". If we allow our children to dawdle through their job half-heartedly, or to rush through it with poor attention to detail, they will not get much satisfaction from it, they will not be proud of themselves and they will not learn all that they are capable of learning. When we require children to do their best, they feel more successful and they grow in confidence, motivation, self-reliance and consideration, as well as becoming more co-operative and less resistant. So for our sakes, as well as for our children's sakes, we need to help them "learn how to learn".

How can we help our children to be successful at school? How can we help them to enjoy challenges and to take pride in doing their best? To achieve these aims we need to consistently guide our children into useful habits.

The following suggestions focus mostly on homework habits for several reasons.

a Productive homework habits enable children to get the most out of their homework.

b The child will take his homework habits with him into school.

c Homework is something parents can influence greatly.

Children think that the purpose of homework is simply to get it over with. As adults, we know that homework assignments serve one or more of the following very important purposes:

- practising, revising or memorising in order to reinforce what has been learned
- exploring a new aspect of a topic
- establishing productive work habits.

In addition, homework can keep parents aware of

- the subject matter
- the school's standards
- how well the child is mastering the subject matter and achieving the school's standards.

Here are the homework routines and rules that will consistently achieve all of the above aims:

1. Your child's brain needs high-quality fuel in order to do high-quality work

Allow only healthy lunches and healthy after-school snacks: low in sugar, salt, fat and refined carbohydrates. Manufacturers know how to make foods very appealing, even addictive: simply load them with hidden sugar, salt and fat. So it is not surprising that children are strongly drawn to the foods that are not good for them. An easy way to reduce hassles and improve your child's brain functioning as well as his willingness and attention to detail is to stop bringing these foods into your home. For guidelines on nutrition, see Chapter 16.

2. Have a sacred homework time every day (except Sundays)

Start the habit of having your child sit down and do homework, memorising or revision *every evening*, even if no homework has been set by the school for the next day. Among other benefits, this is the way to train children and teenagers in the habit of revising well in advance of tests, rather than cramming for one or two nights before a test.

Why is it so important to make a daily homework schedule for your child and to make sure that he sticks to it? Because *routines reduce resistance*. A routine that parents insist upon is a force external to the child. The routine frees the child's mind from two very negative, debilitating emotions:

- the nagging worry (often called "pressure" or "stress") about when, or even if, he will be able to force himself to start his homework, and

- the guilt he feels when he leaves his homework too late to do a good job or when he manages to avoid it altogether.

This combination of anxiety and guilt is very destructive.

Do not skip weekends and holidays. Two or more days in a row without homework can make re-establishing the routines on Monday much more difficult. A break of two days is a long time in the life of a child or teenager. During this time he can mentally start sliding out of the productive habits that you have been putting so much effort into reinforcing during the week.

One day off a week is the optimum. One day off will be greatly appreciated, and it will not undermine the weekly routines. It is wise to designate Sunday as the homework-free day, which means that all weekend homework and revision need to be completed on Saturday. Your child will have the gift of one day a week when no thought of work need enter his mind. This is especially important for the pupil who is not feeling successful.

Your child can have a shorter homework, revision or memorising session during the holidays, but do not let him off. That would be misplaced compassion; it hinders far more than it helps. On all non-school days, set the homework time for *early* in the day to make sure it really happens.

Plan for homework to be done at the same time every day, whenever possible. That way it is predictable and therefore easier for everyone to remember and accept. Of course, this may not always be possible. Modern life has so many variables: after-school activities, parents' work schedules, household tasks, emergencies, etc. But making homework an absolutely clear priority by devoting *some* time to it every day is an important key to school success. Make a chart and post it in a prominent place. Refer to it frequently. This will greatly reduce confusion and resistance.

If the school has not assigned any homework that is due the following day:

- Have your child get a head-start on homework that is due in a few days, rather than allowing him to leave it until the evening before it is due.

- Have him do some revision of a topic that is causing him trouble or some practising of a micro-skill you think he needs to improve. Some examples of micro-skills might be: reading aloud with expression, practising last week's or last term's spelling words, practising handwriting or multiplication facts.

If your child is not yet in the habit of doing some homework every day, you may need to start with short daily sessions. And of course you will need to make sure that the work is easy enough that he experiences satisfaction rather than frustration. Gradually work up to *one or two hours of homework every evening*, depending on the school's guidelines. One hour is usually the minimum time needed in junior school and two hours in senior school, to:

- do a thorough job on homework assignments
- read to a parent
- work a bit every day on special reports, projects or coursework
- revise well in advance for quizzes, tests and exams
- practise a few micro-skills in order to improve weak areas.

3. *Find out from your child's school what the guidelines are in each year for how long homework should take*

The school may say something like: Two subjects each week night and three over the weekend, each to take approximately half an hour. However long the school says that the homework should take, *do not let your child spend longer than the recommended amount of time on it.* This rule is important for a number of reasons:

- The child who wastes time earlier in the evening by complaining or arguing may panic a few hours later and plead to be allowed to stay up past his bedtime to finish. This child may end up with no guilt-free leisure time. He is left with the feeling that all he ever does is school work and homework, even though we know that for a large chunk of his evening he was staring at, rather than actually doing, his homework.
- Some children, particularly those who are sensitive and unconfident, become perfectionists and would choose, if allowed, to spend most of their evening working. This is no good for them; all children need to have "down time" every day.

- A child may be working diligently but find the work so difficult that it takes him longer to finish than it should. He too needs guilt-free leisure time. And the school needs to know that he is not capable of completing the homework within the suggested time. Otherwise, the teachers will continue to set homework that is not appropriate for this child.

State schools are required by law to differentiate the delivery of the curriculum to enable all pupils to learn. The child who spends all evening working should not simply be given less homework. Each of his teachers will need to find out where the difficulty lies and then teach him from that point, rather than expecting him to understand something that he does not yet understand.

When a child attends a highly academic, prestigious school and is just managing to hang in there by spending an inordinate amount of time on homework and revision (and possibly extra tutoring), the parents may be reluctant to reveal the truth to the school. They may worry that the school would conclude that a child who is struggling does not belong there. And the school may be right. This can be a blow to parents, and even to the child, who may blame himself for letting his parents down. When parents are positive and learn to adjust their expectations more realistically, the child will follow suit and take in his stride the move to a more suitable school.

4. Work before play

One of the best ways to help children take homework seriously is to make, and then enforce, the rule that homework and revision need to be completed, *to the parents' satisfaction*, before leisure activities can begin, for example:

- television, computer, video games, etc.
- telephoning or texting friends
- going out
- playing music, etc.

This rule helps ease children into the habit of *earning* the goodies in life, rather than *expecting* instant gratification.

After school, many children do need to unwind and have something to eat before they plunge into their homework. A healthy snack and an *active break* will relax and refresh them: a short bike ride, playing catch, trampolining, etc. Sitting in front of a screen, however, does not refresh or motivate; in fact, it saps enthusiasm for any other activity. Remember that people managed to relax without the help of screens from the dawn of time until about 50 years ago.

5. Eliminate distractions

There should be *no* distractions in the whole house during the sacred homework time. You, the parent, need to be in charge of eliminating all temptations in order to make it easier for your child to concentrate. It is the parent's job to remove all potential distractions, rather than nagging about them. Before the homework even comes out of the school bag:

- Make sure that no screen is on within the child's earshot.
- Put the telephone on answer-phone and turn down the ringer.
- Together with your child, remove all toys and unnecessary equipment from the table.
- Put any pets that might distract in another room.
- If you have a toddler who cannot safely be left in another room, set him up with a highly absorbing activity (one that you bring out only at this time) so that he will not be interrupting the homework session.

6. Train your child to be organised

Disorganisation is very distracting. Do not expect an immature or impulsive or resistant child to know how to organise himself. You will need to train him. Allow on the table at any given time only what the child needs for that step of that task. Do not put his other work away yourself; that is your child's job. Do not tell him where to put things; figuring that out is also his job. Instead, prepare for success by asking leading questions:

- "Where do you want to put your diagram so it won't get wrinkled?"

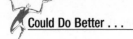

- "Where should you put the highlighter so that you'll know where it is the next time you need it?"
- "How will you keep this section of your project separate from the other section?"

The child may respond to such a question by taking a sensible action, for example by putting the highlighter back in his pencil case. In addition to action, require him to answer your questions in words; this will help the over-arching principles of organisation to sink in to his long-term memory.

7. Build in realistic breaks

Learning can be frustrating and emotionally exhausting for children and teens who are not yet successful learners. To prevent overload, insist that your child has an *active break* (not in front of a screen) every 15-30 minutes, depending on his age and current ability to concentrate on schoolwork. Decide in advance when your child can have breaks. This will, over time, curb the child's tendency to complain or to invent ingenious excuses for getting up and doing something else.

8. Do not let your child leave the hardest task until last

Make sure your child tackles the most troublesome subjects or tasks while his brain is freshest. This will promote optimum learning. It will also remove the nagging dread that eats away at anyone's good humour when they are putting off something that they expect will be unpleasant.

9. Divide each homework task into three distinct stages

This teaches children and teenagers the habit of paying attention to detail and doing their best. Here are the three stages:

Stage One: The parent and the child do a talk-through. In this vital first stage, we bring back into the child's working memory everything that he needs to keep in mind to do the task well and learn whatever there is to learn. We do this through questioning, which is far more effective than telling. Even for simple pieces of work, have him tell you *exactly* what he needs to do and how and why. Ask leading questions to guide him to think carefully about aspects of the task that he may be unaware of or may wish to ignore.

> "How many pages does this essay have to be?"
> "What will you do if you can't spell a word?"
> "Do you have to write full sentences?"
> "Where do you put the carry number?"

The parents' job is to ask the questions; the child's job is to think for himself and to answer the parent's questions. The only time that you would switch from asking him to telling him what to do and how to do it is when one of his answers is incorrect, incomplete or confused. Once the point has been clarified to your satisfaction, ask him the same question again, as many times as necessary, until he can tell you exactly what he needs to do and how he will do it.

Stage Two: The child does the homework, without any help. Homework is designed to be done by the child, not by the parent. With very few exceptions, homework is not meant to be a collaborative effort. Homework should be ongoing training in self-reliance, so in the second stage the child works completely on his own, *with no help*. If you think he might need help with some aspect of his homework, include questions about that in the talk-through. Once Stage Two begins, your child is on his own. A thorough talk-through in Stage One will eliminate many of the mistakes he usually makes, but of course he will make some mistakes. When the child makes a mistake do not say a word, do not frown, nudge, shake your head or point to the mistake.

Until your child is more mature and motivated, I recommend that you stay in the room with him during Stage Two, so that you can Descriptively Praise and Reflectively Listen every few minutes, if necessary (see Chapter 8). But don't answer any questions or even give clues. Stage Two is the child's job.

Stage Three: The last stage is the time when we comment on what the child has produced. Together, the parent and the child evaluate the work.

> **a** First, each of you finds three good things to Descriptively Praise about the piece of work. ***You must not rush this part of***

> ***Stage Three.*** Children learn a great deal from discussion of what they have done *right*.
> Don't let him say, vaguely, "It's OK," or even, "My answers are right," which is a bit more descriptive. Instead, insist that your child be specific. He could say, "I wrote four facts about photosynthesis," or, "I looked up how to spell 'Mediterranean,' so I know it's right".
>
> **b** Then, each of you notice and mention two things about that piece of work that he will need to improve. The more thoroughly you have done the talk-through, the less there will be that needs correcting or improving. Even so, on most days you will probably notice more than two things that could be improved. But mention only two; otherwise you risk discouraging your child. Together, discuss the things that he needs to improve, and have him make those four corrections.

Stage Three is very important, so give it plenty of time. And don't be surprised if your child resists noticing his good work as well as his mistakes. He may be in the habit of thinking his homework is over as soon as he stops writing. Your insistence on Stage Three may come as a shock.

10. Use of computers for homework and projects

Older children will often want, and sometimes actually need, to use the computer for homework and projects. Unsupervised, this can easily degenerate into surreptitious playing of computer games, "chatting" online, e-mailing their friends or surfing the net and then quickly switching the screen back to their homework as soon as you enter the room. One way to prevent this from happening is to keep all screens in areas of the house that you can easily supervise and to take action if you even suspect misuse. In addition, use all the mechanical and electronic methods now available to put various computer functions off limits during the sacred homework time.

You may also need a rule with a consequence. Make and stick to a rule that any misuse of the computer automatically means that the child has not earned the right to use the computer, for homework or for pleasure, for the next few days. Don't feel sorry for him and relent when he complains that the implementation of this rule will result in a detention or the teacher marking his work down. He is the one who broke the rule; he brought that consequence on himself. Equally, don't get angry when he breaks your rule. Some amount of rule breaking is a natural part of growing up. Our responses to rule breaking will determine whether the rule breaking gradually escalates or gradually fades away. Instead of lecturing, "It's your own fault", we can show that we care about the child's feelings: "It sounds like you're worried that you'll get into trouble. You're probably wishing you hadn't broken the computer rule".

Another typical problem is that your child or teenager may print out pages and pages of information from the Internet and hand it in as his own work. At the higher levels of academic study, plagiarism is a crime. Even when that is not a concern, passing off someone else's work as his own allows the child to avoid using his brain and allows him to not take seriously the requirements of the assignment. It is, therefore, the parents' job to require children to put everything in their own words. Expect resistance at first.

When this has been a problem, the solutions are:

During Stage One (the talk-through):

- By asking questions, not by telling, guide your child to understand why he should not pass off another person's work as his own. You want him to realise that it is wrong to take credit for what another person has produced.
- He also needs to understand that one of the teacher's purposes, in setting the class a particular essay or project, is to give pupils practice in learning to think for themselves. Printing out someone else's work is the opposite of thinking for himself.
- Decide for yourself whether the computer is necessary for this piece of homework. Do not take your child's word for it.
- To teach him what to do instead of handing in someone else's work as his own, require your child or teenager to think about and jot down an outline of what he will write. Once he realises that he has a fair idea of the key points he needs to cover, he

will be more confident and therefore less tempted to pad his essay or project with reams of someone else's work.

- Make sure he knows that in Stage Three (the improving stage) you will be checking to see that he has put everything from the textbook or the Internet into his own words, not just changed a phrase here and there.

During Stage Three: Check to see whether he has written about the key points that he jotted down during the talk-through, and whether he has used his own words.

Homework Profile

The following questions will help you to see more clearly what is working well in your homework routines and what needs to be improved.

1 What does you child do between arriving home from school and starting homework?
2 What does your child eat between breakfast and homework time?
3 How does each homework session begin?
4 Who initiates the homework session and how?
5 What are the usual beginning and ending times for homework:
   - on school nights?
   - on weekends and holidays?
6 How many school nights each week do you supervise homework?
7 How many weekend days do you supervise homework?
8 How long is each homework session?
9 How much of that time are you actively involved in supervision?
10 What do you *do* when supervising homework?
11 What do you *not do* when supervising homework?
12 How do you deal with your child's uncomfortable feelings?
13 How do you deal with your child's negative actions (or lack of action)?
14 What homework rules do you stand absolutely firm on?
15 What homework rules are you flexible about and in what way?
16 How does the homework session end?

17 What are the rewards for co-operation, doing his best, satisfactory results?

18 What are the consequences for non-compliance, not doing his best, poor results?

Chapter 8

Reinforcing the homework routines and rules

Consistency

Consistent routines and rules enable the child to feel comfortable because his environment is predictable and therefore emotionally safe. Consistent means unvarying, non-negotiable, inflexible.

A parent may not want to live with consistent routines and rules because they are as binding on the parent as they are on the child. Consistency limits our freedom to be spontaneous.

But consistency is what children need. This especially applies to the sensitive, intense, emotionally immature child, whose natural rhythms are often quite inconsistent. He needs our help to get and stay on an even keel. The child who is constantly wangling for an exception is the very child who cannot handle exceptions well. He gets hooked on trying to get away with minor or major misbehaviour. He stores the inconsistencies in his long-term memory and uses them as ammunition to try and get us to change our minds the next time.

The easy-going, laid-back child is more able to deal with some exceptions and changes to the established routines. He takes these in his stride. But a lack of clarity and consistency adversely affects even the relatively easy child. He too can become an arch manipulator if parents say one thing and do another.

When routines and rules are not consistent, far too much of a child's energies go into testing, arguing, wheedling for exceptions and splitting hairs. Paradoxically, consistent rules and routines free children by allowing them to put more thought and energy into their primary developmental task, which is learning in its broadest sense: noticing, experimenting, making inferences, drawing conclusions, and applying to new situations the knowledge they have gained.

Consistency has the added benefit of depersonalising parental requirements. The child can see that the parent is not making up a rule on the spur of the moment out of anger or anxiety. He learns to accept even an unwelcome restriction with a rather philosophical attitude of "Oh well, this is the way life is", almost as if the rule were a force of nature, beyond anyone's control.

Follow-through

At any given moment during the daily homework session, a child is either co-operating with the routines and rules or he is not co-operating. We need to stay consistent when little bits of minor misbehaviour start to surface. Otherwise our children will not take us seriously about the major misbehaviour.

Follow-through is a term that refers to how we respond to the instances of co-operation or its opposite. When we think about follow-through, our minds usually focus automatically on consequences for misbehaviour. But I want to start by discussing how we can effectively follow-through when the child *has co-operated*. We need to regularly follow through after good behaviour because that is the most effective method of reinforcing co-operation, motivation and self-reliance.

However, quite often parents ignore good behaviour. When a child is doing the right thing, we often grab the opportunity to turn our attention to something else that needs doing. Even a child who is frequently resistant about homework will occasionally make a real effort, or will do what you say the first time you say it. Often parents take these positive actions for granted because they believe that this level of co-operation is no more than they have a right to expect from the child. This is an understandable reaction, but it is short-sighted. Until the child is co-operative, motivated and self-reliant *most of the time*, we cannot simply expect it. We must reinforce it to achieve it. Often parents report that they hesitate to point out to their child what he has done right, in case

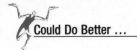

that reminds the child that he could be acting up. That does happen on rare occasions, especially with a very impulsive child and especially in the early weeks. But that is not a good enough reason to abandon following-through for positive behaviour.

We cannot expect our children to simply accept our new routines and rules. Changing habits is difficult even for adults. This is true even when we are absolutely convinced that a new habit would be good for us (for example, eating healthily or exercising). Children, however, are not at all convinced that the new homework habits will benefit them, and they are naturally reluctant to concentrate more carefully on an area of their lives where they do not currently feel comfortable or successful.

There are several very powerful tools that parents can use to help children and teenagers to overcome this very understandable resistance. One of these is Descriptive Praise. It can be used many times every day, and the more you use it, the more quickly the new homework habits will be established.

The type of praise we generally give our children is called "evaluative", for example:

"Well done!" "Good boy!" "You're so clever!" "That's wonderful!"

We often give this praise to help our children feel confident or to encourage them to keep trying. One problem with this over-the-top type of praise is that our children do not believe us. They can see that the rest of the world doesn't think they are so wonderful. Therefore they conclude one of two things: either that we do not really believe that they are amazingly clever and talented but are exaggerating to try and make them feel good or that we do believe all the superlatives simply because we love them.

Descriptive Praise, however, is a very different kind of praise. Descriptive Praise is the most powerful motivator I know. It helps children want to improve and it gives them the information they need about what to do in order to improve. Descriptive Praise consists of leaving out the evaluative praise altogether and simply noticing and mentioning every tiny step in the right direction:

- small improvements in behaviour, attitude, work habits,
  attention to detail, social skills, etc.
- behaviour or work that is not wonderful or terrific but just OK
  (actions that you might ordinarily take for granted)
- the absence of the negative behaviour.

At first you may be worried that your children will not realise you are
praising them, without the addition of "Well done" or "That's terrific".
They will know because you will be talking about what they did right,
your face will look pleased and your tone of voice will sound pleased.

Descriptive Praise is so motivating because it taps into a universal truth
about humans: all of us (even children, even teenagers) are disposed to
want to please the people who are pleasant to us. When I talk of being
pleasant to our children I do not mean indulging them or giving in; I
mean showing our appreciation and approval, being friendly and polite.
In addition, all children desperately want their parents to be proud of
them. With Descriptive Praise, even those children and teenagers who
had given up trying to please start to feel better and behave better.

Here are some examples of Descriptive Praise which can motivate a
reluctant child or teenager to accept the new routines. Each Descriptive
Praise takes only a few seconds to utter:

Following instructions

- "You did exactly what I told you to do."
- "You took your books out as soon as I asked. No time-wasting!"
- "Thanks for not arguing."

Following routines and rules

- "You're following the new routine, and you didn't need any
  reminders. That shows maturity."
- "You told yourself the right thing to do and then you did it.
  That's self-reliance."
- "You're remembering the new rule."

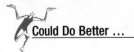

Staying on task

- "Instead of giving up when it got hard, you re-read the instructions. Very sensible."
- "I see you've been sitting for ten minutes, without once getting up."
- "You've stopped tapping the table. It's much more peaceful now."
- "You're still writing, even though that noise is distracting."

Paying attention to details

- "You noticed your own mistake. And you're correcting it without my having to tell you to."
- "You've written four sentences, and three of them start with a capital letter. You're remembering the rule."
- "The directions said to answer in full sentences, and you did, even though it takes longer."
- "Every letter in this word is sitting exactly on the line."
- "There is no clutter on this desk."

Politeness and consideration

- "You're using your indoor voice."
- "Thanks for looking right at me while I'm talking to you."
- "You're waiting patiently."
- "I appreciate that you didn't interrupt me."
- "You might be feeling annoyed, but all I hear are polite words."

Positive attitudes

- "You weren't sure how to answer that comprehension question, but you had a go. That was brave."
- "You didn't say 'I don't know'. You took a sensible guess."
- "You're not complaining."

When we frequently show that we are pleased, our children see that they can please us. The more we notice and mention the positive behaviour, attitudes and work habits, the more co-operative, motivated and self-reliant our children will become.

Start with ten Descriptive Praises per day, per child. You will soon find that it feels so good (for the parent as well as the child) and is so motivating that soon you will be Descriptively Praising easily ten times each hour.

Rewards

At first, when children are just learning the habit of co-operation, they often become more motivated to improve when an incentive is provided. The incentive serves to get them started. Parents generally understand that a well-chosen reward can help overcome a child's resistance. But parents may worry that rewarding a child for doing the right thing will spiral out of control and create a monster, a child who is willing to co-operate only if the reward is sufficiently appealing. In fact, the very opposite turns out to be true. As the new habit or behaviour becomes firmly established, rewards can easily be reduced and then eliminated.

The best rewards are those which are easy and quick to deliver and cost nothing. That way you will be willing and able to dole out many little rewards every day, not just for wonderful behaviour and work habits (which you will not see every day) but for small improvements, even when the results are still not quite what you were hoping for. The very easiest, quickest and most effective rewards are our positive reactions to every little improvement:

- Smiles
- Hugs
- Descriptive Praise
- Thumbs-up sign or other gesture of approval.

These tiny rewards will take you a long way. They are food for our children's souls, as vital for them to have every day as is the food for their bodies that we give them every day.

In order to help your child develop the habit of doing his best, notice all the tiny steps in the right direction and reward them immediately with these four easy, quick rewards. For example when he:

- Co-operates when you ask him to show you what his homework is.
- Does not argue when you point out a mistake.
- Does not ask if he can watch T.V. before homework.
- Explains to you the worked example in his text book, instead of ignoring it.
- Does not say, "This is boring".

Some parents believe that pocket money should be earned; others feel that pocket money is the child's right. Some favour a combination. My experience is that children and teenagers who have to "earn" most of their treats become more motivated, more appreciative and more responsible. So if you are keen to improve some aspects of your child's behaviour or work habits, and money happens to be important to him, it seems a waste of a resource *not* to use money as a motivator. If you choose to use pocket money as an incentive, it is advisable to reward daily, by means of a chart, even if you only hand over the money weekly. Be willing to start by targeting very small improvements, if necessary. Achievements such as bringing home the right books and sitting down at the agreed time to do his homework could earn small amounts of money.

Be aware that using money as a reward may not work if your child has a stash of cash in his bedroom or a bankcard and an account full of birthday money.

With consistent rewards for small bits of good behaviour, your child will soon see that co-operation pays off. He realises, although he cannot articulate it, that the more good things he does, the more access he has to the goodies in life. As soon as children realise this vital fact of life, they become very motivated to co-operate.

Depending on several factors, it may take your child a few days or a few weeks to come to this important realisation. It will happen sooner if:

- Your child has a relatively easy-going temperament to begin with.
- His self-esteem is relatively intact.
- You supervise his homework, reading, revision and projects closely.

- You stay calm and friendly when your child is unco-operative or argumentative, rather than resorting to the old, ineffective strategies of arguing back, lecturing, nagging and shouting.
- You focus your attention and your comments on the tiny improvements, rather than on the huge problems that remain.
- You are generous with your smiles, hugs, Descriptive Praise and small signs of approval and appreciation.

However, it will take longer, up to a month, for your child to see the clear connection between his good behaviour and the possible rewards if:

- He has a sensitive, intense, impulsive temperament.
- He feels like a failure ("I'm dumb", "I'm bad").
- He is angry or irritable a lot of the time.
- The work he is being given at school is too difficult for him.
- Parents are not united about the homework routines and rules.

Your child may *never* make this important realisation if you skimp on the Descriptive Praise and the tiny rewards or if he is still getting told off a lot.

Once a child realises that co-operation pays off, you will find that he does more and more of the right things. And he starts making an effort to refrain from doing the wrong things. At this point you can move to medium-sized rewards for several consecutive days (and eventually for a whole week) of the new, positive behaviour or work habits. These slightly larger rewards will motivate your child even more to keep up and even expand the new, positive behaviours and habits. But do not expect a child, even a teenager, to be motivated to work for a reward that is more than a week away. Big, long-term rewards (such as a new bike for a whole term's worth of not getting sent to the head or getting B's on the weekly spelling tests) are rarely motivating enough *by themselves*. Even though the child may be desperate for the reward, the future dream cannot compete with his present immaturity and impulsivity. He needs to get into *daily* good habits so concentrate your attention on the tiny daily rewards and on the medium-sized rewards. They are the real motivators. Don't even mention the big reward of a new bike or guitar or ice skates or trip to Legoland. Let the big reward be a completely unexpected bonus at the end of a term full of daily improvements that you have rewarded daily and weekly.

To choose the medium-sized rewards, just recall any activity or treat that your child has especially enjoyed or has asked for. You can get creative with these slightly larger rewards; imagine what your child might enjoy. Here are some examples of rewards that have worked well to motivate children and teenagers to improve all aspects of their behaviour and school work. You will see that these rewards are easy to arrange, either completely free or inexpensive and often enjoyable for the parent as well.

1 Being brought breakfast in bed.
2 Choosing the menu for a meal and shopping with you for the ingredients.
3 An extra story or song at bedtime.
4 Ten minutes of rough-and-tumble with a parent.
5 A candle-light dinner.
6 A snack in a café.
7 Trying on Mum's jewellery or Dad's ties.
8 Playing cards or a board game with a parent.
9 Ten extra minutes
    – at the park
    – in bed after the alarm goes off in the morning
    – of screen time
    – staying up after bedtime
    – of Quality Time with a parent.
10 Having a friend to stay the night.
11 Joining in an adult activity with a parent, such as cooking or DIY.
12 Going window-shopping with a parent.
13 Camping out or having a picnic in the garden.
14 Sleeping in the sitting room.
15 Playing make-believe with a parent.
16 Playing in the garden in the rain.
17 Handing the money to the cashier and receiving the change at the supermarket.
18 Stopping for five minutes in front of the pet shop window to look at the puppies.
19 A bath in the dark.
20 Going somewhere just with you, without siblings.

There are some important guidelines that can help you to use rewards most effectively:

1   Parents are apt to make the mistake of giving children too much too easily: toys, sports equipment, treats, electronics, money, after-school activities, clothes, etc. Children are given these things as their birthright, usually with no strings attached. But every so often, when children misbehave, furious parents who are at their wits' end try to claw back some of these rights, or they threaten to. By doing this, or by threatening it, the parents hope that the child will realise the seriousness of the situation, will see that the parents mean business and will be motivated to improve his ways. It rarely works that way. In fact, the child is outraged because he was not told in the first place that access to these goodies was conditional on a certain standard of behaviour or academic performance. As far as the child is concerned, the parents have changed the rules in the middle of the game, which is always perceived as grossly unfair. Instead of parents handing children all these goodies on a plate (which often results in a careless, unappreciative attitude), I suggest that children be required to earn most of what they currently take for granted.

2   Make the task easy enough that the child will be able to earn the reward with a bit more effort than usual, rather than by having to be "really, really good". He probably cannot manage a huge improvement all at once. But with time and rewards and a healthy lifestyle (see Section IV), he will surprise you. He will become ever more willing and more able to control himself.

3   Do not take away (or even threaten to take away) rewards that he has already earned, no matter how angry you become over subsequent misbehaviour. Once he has earned it, the reward is his. Otherwise, the child with poor impulse-control will lose his hard-earned rewards and will soon give up even trying to improve.

4   Occasionally announce that an unexpected reward is earnable. For example, you might arrange to play with him for ten minutes as soon as he has memorised his spelling words or after twenty minutes of doing his maths without complaining. In addition to the rewards that a child knows well in advance are available, it is also very motivating

for the child to be surprised by rewards that he was not expecting. This helps the child to see himself in a new light, as a person who can delight and please the parent. It also models a very generous, giving attitude on our part, which the child will, over time, absorb and mirror back.

5   Children, particularly the more sensitive, intense, impulsive ones, are often asking us for something, directly or indirectly:

"Can I play on the computer?"
"Will you fix this for me?"
"Can I have another biscuit?"
"Will you play with me?"
"I can't get this to stay on. You do it."
"I never get the Mickey Mouse cup."
"Can I wear this to the party?"

If you want to respond to a particular request with a "Yes", it is helpful to turn your reply into an instant reward that reinforces the homework habits you value. You could say:

"Yes I'd be glad to help you because you really slowed down and were so careful with your handwriting today. You kept most of your letters on the line."

"Yes, I'll be happy to take the time to sit down and fix this for you. I want to because I'm so pleased with how you've been co-operating about homework. You thought you couldn't do tens-and-units, but you tried and you tried and you didn't give up. And you got most of them right."

6   Do not let your child choose a reward that requires you to do something for him that is his responsibility (such as dressing himself) or his job (such as setting the table or feeding the cat).

7   Similarly, do not let him choose a reward that would get him out of doing something he finds difficult or uncomfortable, such as going to Cubs (if that is problematic) or sharing.

8   Do not expect rewards, by themselves, to motivate a reluctant, impulsive or angry child. A reward is just one tool, a "sweetener", something that makes it somewhat easier for him to drift into the habit of co-operation and self-reliance.

9 When your child does not earn a reward, be disappointed rather than angry or blaming. "What a shame! I was hoping we could have an extra story tonight" is more motivating than, "It's your own fault! You wasted time by arguing when you should have been concentrating."

10 Do not use food as a reward. Food is too emotive an issue, too symbolic of love and nurturing and acceptance.

To summarise: when we use rewards to motivate, at first the child co-operates because receiving the praise and rewards feels good. Quite soon co-operation starts to become a habit. Eventually the child chooses to do the right thing because he feels better about himself as a person when he does. This is the birth of conscience.

Now let us turn our attention to following through when the child is resisting being co-operative. Before I discuss consequences, here is a very useful technique that often (but not always) helps a resistant child to be much less resistant.

Reflective listening

This technique motivates children and overcomes resistance by helping them to see the parent as an ally, rather than as the enemy. It also repairs damage to self-esteem and self-confidence. Reflective Listening is not always easy to master, but it is very effective. You will find that you use it many times every day. The benefits of Reflective Listening are that it helps the angry or anxious child to feel heard and understood. This can defuse uncomfortable emotions and potentially explosive situations. The child starts to relax and no longer feels that he needs to act up in order to make a point or get the parents' attention. At this point he often automatically turns his attention towards problem-solving. Over time, Reflective Listening teaches children and teenagers a vocabulary for expressing their feelings in words, rather than through tantrums, whingeing or misbehaviour.

Reflective Listening has five steps.

Step 1: You consciously set aside your completely understandable feelings of frustration, guilt, confusion or despair. This step is not always easy to achieve, but it becomes much easier when we remember that it is not the child's fault that he is being resistant. He has drifted into bad habits because his difficulties have not yet been properly addressed. "Fault" is a concept that usually implies deliberate wrong-doing. It is worth stating emphatically that in this situation *no one* is at fault, not the child or teenager, not parents, not teachers. Once parents and teachers have a more complete understanding of the causes of a child's lack of school success, they often feel deep regret and remorse for the angry, accusatory things they have said in the past to the child.

Step 2: You stop what you are doing and listen attentively. The child may be complaining, whingeing, arguing or even crying. Sometimes he is silent but his facial expression and body language speak volumes: a scowl of fury, a dejected slouch, brows knit in worry. You can show you are listening by responding with: "Oh…. Mmm…. I see….". This helps the child start to relax and feel safe, whereas asking, "What's the matter?" often puts an inarticulate child on the spot and results in a shrug and "I don't know," or possibly a torrent of blame.

Step 3: You imagine what your child is feeling below the level of his words.

- "This is stupid" often means "This worksheet looks too hard".
- "Go away" or "Don't look at me" or "Leave me alone" might mean "I'm afraid I will lose my temper if you keep talking to me" or possibly "I'm ashamed that I keep making mistakes".
- "I hate maths" could really mean "I don't understand what the teacher says, and she gets annoyed with me if I ask".

Step 4: You reflect back to the child in words what you imagine he is feeling, rather than trying to argue him out of his version of reality.

- "I can see you're angry. It's hard to settle down to homework when you'd rather be playing."

- "It looks like you're dreading the idea of getting started on your project."
- "Maybe you're feeling that this maths is just too difficult and that you'll never understand it."
- "Even just thinking about revision is getting you down."

Step 5 is optional: You give your child his wishes in fantasy. This often lightens the mood, and again it shows the child that you care and understand:

- "You probably wish you would never ever, ever have another spelling test again in your whole life."
- "What if you had a magical essay-writing pen that did all the work for you!"
- "I wish I could make time fly so that you would be finished with your homework in three seconds."

When a child is experiencing uncomfortable emotions, he often acts this out through subtle or not-so-subtle misbehaviour: arguing, complaining, time-wasting, refusing, breaking his pencil, storming off, etc. Knowing this, we can choose to respond initially with Reflective Listening whenever the child is unco-operative, rather than by nagging, arguing back or shouting, which are all quite counter-productive and emotionally draining for the parent as well as the child.

Consequences

If we want our children to respect us and to take our routines and rules seriously, we need to respond immediately to *all* instances of non-co-operation. This means not only the major but also the minor infractions, not only the deliberate misbehaviour but also the impulsive, compulsive and habitual, not only the breaking of rules but also the bending of rules.

When parents have not yet discovered the almost magical power of consistency, they tend to apply sanctions in a rather haphazard manner, based on their mood, or on how tired they are that day, or on how upset they already are about something else. Sadly, they do not realise that inconsistent parental responses often perpetuate misbehaviour. The parents end up assuming that consequences don't work for their child.

Parents are often reluctant to follow through consistently after misbehaviour because they believe that more consequences will result in even more whingeing, sulking, tears, tantrums, refusals and verbal aggression. That is occasionally true in the first week or so. Sometimes things do get worse before the get better. So persevere!

Sometimes parents are hesitant to be consistent because they worry that they would come across as harsh, tyrannical or uncaring. When we choose, for these reasons or for any other, to ignore subtle or minor misbehaviour, the child gradually loses respect for what we say, which results in more and more unco-operative behaviour. Parents try to be patient, but eventually they snap, reacting with blame, threats and shouting. Ironically, parental reluctance to immediately address each incident results in parents speaking and acting in negative, unfriendly ways that children *do* often perceive as harsh, tyrannical or uncaring. Erratic consequences are more likely to breed resentment and anxiety, whilst consistent consequences soon lead to a more relaxed, more confident, motivated, better-behaved child or teenager.

Consequences are most effective when they are mild, when they are over with quickly and when they happen every time a rule is broken. The first rule for parents is: *Take immediate action.* Action means doing, not saying. So do not repeat yourself or remind, cajole, threaten, argue or bargain. All of those responses will only prolong the problem.

Here are some consequences that parents have used successfully to help transform homework habits:

1   Paradoxically, when a child is sitting in front of his homework not working properly or not working at all, whether he is complaining or staring into space for long minutes at a time, a useful action is to remove his books, paper, pencil case and any other equipment. You might think the child would be delighted with this turn of events and interpret your action as letting him off the hook. Interesting, the opposite is true. When the space in front of him on the homework table is suddenly empty, he cannot continue to fool himself that he is doing his homework. It soon hits home that there is no longer a grey area where he can pretend to himself that he is working. It is

important for parents not to threaten this. Instead, prepare for success earlier in the day by having several talk-throughs, during which you explain, and then have your child repeat back to you, exactly what will happen if you judge that he is not working properly. Then take immediate action, as soon as necessary.

Remember that, deep down, children want to please parents who are friendly and appreciative. So if you have committed yourself to rewarding all the tiny bits of good behaviour with Descriptive Praise and smiles, your child will soon be motivated to do the right thing.

Do not be tempted to give him back his books as soon as he promises to follow your instructions or to do his work carefully. Instead, wait until you can see, from his tone of voice, his facial expression, and even his posture, that he is completely ready to do his best. Do yet another talk-through. Have him tell you exactly what he will do and how he will do it. Getting to this point may take longer than you wish it would. Very occasionally a stubborn child will waste so much time before he is ready to co-operate that the homework will not get completed within the allotted time. Do not let him work any later that evening, for the reasons I explained in Chapter 7. Send a note in to the teacher briefly explaining what you did, and let your child take whatever consequence the school gives him. Above all, stay positive. Children learn quickly from consequences when we stay calm and don't blame. But as soon as we get angry, or even annoyed, the child gets angry right back and is no longer motivated to do what he knows he should do.

2   An *Action Replay* is a particularly useful consequence for misbehaviour that is impulsive, compulsive or habitual (but it is not usually effective for deliberate misbehaviour, as it requires a degree of willingness). In an Action Replay the scene is replayed, but this time the child says or does the right thing. For example, if he called you a name, this time he says how he feels, just as strongly, but using polite words. If he threw his pencil across the room, in the Action Replay he will handle his frustration more maturely, perhaps by making a request for a short break or by taking several deep breaths. If he was

saying "I'm stupid", in the Action Replay he has another go at the sum that seems too difficult; this time he takes a sensible guess.

3   If we shift our focus from indulging to rewarding, a very effective consequence would be that the child has not earned his reward. For example, the rule might be that he can earn an hour of screen time every evening by completing his homework within the allotted time. If he wastes time and therefore does not complete the homework *to your satisfaction*, he has not earned that evening's screen time. For the child, this is not the same as a withdrawal of his entitlement to screen time. With the new way he cannot take it for granted that he will be able to go on the computer every evening; he knows that he must earn it daily. (If the homework he is set is too difficult for him to complete within the allotted time, see Chaper 9).

The tools that I have described in this chapter are not magic wands. But over time, and sooner than you would imagine, these follow-through techniques will help improve your child's co-operation, confidence, motivation, self-reliance and consideration.

CHAPTER 9

Overcoming your child's resistance to the new routines and rules

All children sometimes complain about homework and sometimes look for excuses to put it off until later. The real problems arise when children *habitually* resist doing their best, or resist doing homework altogether. Parents want to understand why their child regularly makes a fuss about doing homework or takes a long time to settle down, and they want to know what they can do to foster willingness and improve concentration. It is worth taking the time to see which of the following reasons apply, as that will help us identify the solutions:

a The child may be motivated to do his homework, but regularly finds that the work is genuinely too difficult for him. He resists in an understandable attempt to avoid frustration, embarrassment and feeling like a failure.

b The child is quite capable of doing a good job on his homework, but only after the parent has explained the instructions or has briefly re-taught some of the concepts.

c He may be able to do his homework but is not self-confident so he assumes he cannot do it. This child is often a perfectionist with a sensitive temperament. He would rather be told off for making a fuss than risk disappointing his parents or teachers by getting it wrong.

d He may be able to do his homework but is just trying to get out of doing it; he knows from past experience that if he makes enough of a fuss his parents will sometimes give in and he will end up working less and playing more.

e He may understand the work and be capable of giving very reasonable verbal responses, but he is trying to avoid writing,

which he finds difficult to do well, very time-consuming or even physically painful.

f Your child may know how to do his work but is not in the habit of doing his best.

g Your child may have picked up from you some subtle clues that you secretly believe the teacher is not worthy of respect.

Of course, there will occasionally be times when you are not sure whether your child cannot or will not do his homework properly. Take the time to discover his current level of mastery.

Here are guidelines for addressing and rectifying each of the above reasons:

a What to do when you can clearly see that the homework is often too difficult for your child:

- Reflectively Listen to your child about how this situation makes him feel (See Chapter 8).
- Do not do his thinking or any of the work for him. That would mask the problem.
- Do not simply require him to do less of it. That would not address the real problem, which is that he needs to master certain skills.
- Make a unilateral decision to simplify the homework so that he can be and feel successful, but do *not* let him just leave it undone. For a child with good listening comprehension whose reading skills are still weak, you can often make the homework do-able by reading aloud to him the instructions, worksheet or textbook passage. As you read each sentence aloud, slowly, with exaggerated expression, require your child first to follow along with his finger, and then to re-read each sentence aloud correctly by himself, as you slowly point to each word.
  He will be able to achieve this quite easily because the words he has just heard you read will still be very fresh in his mind. At first, he may be parroting most of the sentence, rather than actually decoding, but this technique serves several very useful purposes:
  - Seeing and hearing the words simultaneously will soon improve your child's reading skills.

- He will experience himself as a reader, which will enhance his confidence and motivation.
- He will stay actively involved in his homework, rather than sitting back and expecting you to explain it to him.

- Give him lots of practice at an easier level and Descriptively Praise even tiny improvements.

- Make sure that the teachers know when your child is experiencing problems and how you are tackling them. For example, if you are reading the homework instructions aloud to your child, you need to make sure his teachers know this, or else they will continue to expect more of him than he is currently capable of producing.

- Be an effective advocate for your child: learn everything you can about the possible causes of his academic problems and about useful strategies for home and school, and then share what you have learned with his teachers (without directly telling them what to do).

b If the child often seems to need to have certain points clarified or re-taught, parents often jump to incorrect conclusions. It can be tempting to blame the teacher for not having explained the homework properly. This assumption will not hold water if others in the class *do* understand how to do the homework. You may blame your child for not having bothered to listen carefully during the lesson. Here are some likely reasons why a child might not listen carefully to the teacher:

- He may be easily distracted by background noise. This pupil is, in fact, listening as carefully as he currently knows how to listen, given the many auditory and visual distractions of a busy classroom. The child with this problem may complain that his classmates are too noisy and may even blame the teacher for not knowing how to keep the class quiet.

- He may be relatively immature or impulsive and therefore find it difficult to sustain attention on a topic that does not particularly interest him.

- He may be a kinaesthetic learner who pays attention best when he is actively involved but finds it hard to sustain attention when he must sit still and passively take in information.
- He may not be able to process the information as quickly as the teacher is talking, which is one of the signs of an auditory processing problem. Once he loses the thread, the teacher's words become confusing or meaningless, and can seem boring.
- He may not know how to focus on the important details of what the teacher is saying. This child may be able to regale you with statistics or examples but miss the main points of the lesson. He, too, may become confused and bored; soon his mind wanders.
- He may not understand the subject terminology, which once again results in confusion and boredom, as well as a belief that the subject or topic is too hard.
- He may not have really mastered the previous lessons on this topic, so he does not have the foundation with which to make sense of the new information. Without even realising it, he switches off.

Or the child may have no problem with listening, but very quickly forgets what he hears.

The child may regularly arrive home not knowing exactly what his homework is:

- He may have mislaid his homework diary, due to poor organisational skills.
- He may have deliberately left it at school.
- He may have copied down the homework incompletely from the board because he cannot copy accurately or fast enough.
- He may have written down the teacher's oral instructions incorrectly because he cannot easily listen, understand and write all at the same time.

Firstly, parents will need to take responsibility for helping the school to maximise the likelihood that an impulsive, distractible child will be able to pay attention in class. Ask all of his teachers to pay special attention to where this child sits:

- Seat him near the teacher's desk, but included as part of the regular class seating (so that he does not feel singled out).
- Seat him very near (if possible surround him with) positive role models, preferably those with high status in the classroom. He will start to see himself as one of them, and just as importantly, some of that high status will rub off on him in the eyes of his classmates.
- Avoid auditory and visual distractions:
    - Flickering striplights
    - Air conditioners or heaters
    - Doors or windows
    - High traffic areas
    - Pet corner, nature table, Wendy house, etc.
- Arrange a "stimuli-reduced study area", for example a desk that is visually separated from the rest of the classroom by bookshelves. To avoid stigma, the teacher should allow all the pupils to use this area from time to time.

When children have real difficulty writing the homework down accurately or fast enough, parents will need to be advocates for their child to ensure that the teacher takes appropriate action. The teacher might:

- Write the homework instructions in the child's homework diary for him.
- Give the child written homework instructions for him to copy into his homework diary. This will probably be much easier for him than copying from the board, which requires a continual big shift in visual focus as the board is much farther away.
- At the very least, write the homework instructions on the board much earlier in the lesson, so that the child has more time to copy neatly and accurately, rather than having to rush to get it all copied in the last few minutes before the bell rings.

A child who regularly forgets to bring home his homework diary, worksheets and books can learn to remember, although at first he may not believe he can. Teachers can help a dreamy or impulsive pupil to get into the habit of remembering to take home what he needs. Rewards are often very effective.

We should not be surprised or shocked that some children have developed the habit of deliberately leaving their homework at school or conveniently misplacing it. These are children who experience homework as an ordeal to be avoided at all costs. When parents start to establish enjoyable, productive homework routines, it becomes easier and easier for the child to do the right thing.

Sometimes when a child asks for help he wants an explanation of how to do something, but sometimes he actually wants the parent to tell him the answer. He is hoping that the parent's brain will do the work, probably because the parent has done too much for him in the past. We must not fall into the trap of doing our child's thinking for him. Also, do not let him leave any answers blank. He needs to take a guess and write something, even if he is not sure whether his answer is right. Only then can the teacher assess where he is going wrong. Also, do not urge your child to ask the teacher for help. Many children with school problems are too embarrassed to ask. Or else they know from past experience that the teacher's explanation will not clarify matters sufficiently.

When you yourself do not understand the subject or topic, you will not be able to supply your child with the information he wants. This is actually a good thing because information about school subjects is not what children need from their parents. Children need parents who require them to think for themselves *all the time*.

So whenever you feel the urge to explain; do the following instead:

- Ask leading questions, rather than telling your child. Only when his brain has to come up with the answer is he learning.
- Draw pictures and diagrams, using a minimum of words, because, as we have seen, many children with school problems are strong visual learners and weak auditory learners.
- Give lots of examples so that your child can see for himself what they all have in common.
- Reflectively Listen to his frustration and confusion.
- Descriptively Praise him whenever he thinks for himself.

Specifically for mathematics:

- Talk him through a different sum from the one he has to do for his homework. That way, once he understands the principle or procedure from your explanation, he will still have to use his own brain to work out the sum he was given for homework.
- Give examples that use much, much easier numbers so that the child can concentrate solely on the procedures or principles.

c What to do when you know that your child is able to do a particular type or level of homework but he thinks he can't or is simply trying to wriggle out of it because he has managed to in the past:

- Reflectively Listen about his anxieties and his lack of confidence or his resentments.
- Prepare for success by talking through, several times a day, the new plan, which is that in Stage One you will make sure he remembers everything he needs to know, and in Stage Two he will need to do all of his homework on his own, and you will not get angry if he makes mistakes. You can do a short talk-through over breakfast, another talk-through on the way to school, another on the way home from school, and another right before the homework session.
- Remember, he *can* do it. Do not simplify the homework or do part of it for him "to get him started" or even read the instructions to him. That would send him the message that you do not think him capable.
- Do not allow him to do less.
- Stay positive and friendly as you insist that he does it.
- Give lots of Descriptive Praise, especially for willingness, courage and determination.

d What to do when your child understands what to do and how to do it but often tries to avoid writing, which he finds painful, difficult, or time-consuming:

- Recognise that some children find writing physically and therefore emotionally uncomfortable (see Chapter 5).
- Reflectively Listen to how he feels about writing, about schoolwork, homework, his teachers, his abilities, etc.

- He and you may need several sessions with an occupational therapist, who will show you exercises for him to do at home every day to:
    - strengthen his muscles
    - improve his posture, the position of his arms and the way he holds his pencil
    - form his letters correctly.

  The occupational therapist will also tell you if your child would benefit from specially-adapted equipment, such as a wedge-shaped board to place his work on or a moulded pencil grip that guides his fingers into a more comfortable and more effective position.

- With daily, closely supervised practice (no more than 5-10 minutes a day) and lots of Descriptive Praise and Reflective Listening, all children can improve their handwriting and their experience of writing.

- A few children have such severe problems with writing that they should be allowed to do their homework on the computer as soon as they can master keyboard skills. Using a computer can be very liberating for many children with poor fine-motor control, although they may also have some difficulty learning to use a keyboard. On the computer they are often able to express themselves in page after page of creative writing, instead of being limited to the few stilted, awkward sentences they can write by hand within the allotted homework time. When these children are freed from having to think about controlling their pencil to make their handwriting legible, they have more room in their brain to pay attention to spelling, punctuation and capital letters, as well as to plot development and vocabulary. But these children should still practise the micro-skills of handwriting for five or ten minutes every day.

- Every day Descriptively Praise his willingness, patience and determination and every tiny improvement.

e What to do when your child understands his homework and how to do it but regularly rushes through his work, or dawdles his way through it, not doing his best:

- He will need to improve his attention to detail in one or possibly all of the following areas:
  - accuracy
  - thoroughness
  - presentation.
- Expect your child to argue and complain:

  "This is science, so spelling doesn't matter."

  "The teacher doesn't care if it's neat as long as the answer is right."

  "You're not my teacher."

  "I don't have time to write that much."

  "It doesn't say 'complete sentences.'"

  "You think I have to be perfect."

  "I'll miss 'The Simpsons.'"

  Sometimes complaints are phrased as questions, the favourites being: "Why do I have to?" and, "What does it matter?" These are not really questions that your child wants answers to. Remember that you are in charge. Your standard, not the child's and not even the school's, is what your child needs to be striving to reach. So don't argue back. Instead, Reflectively Listen to how he might be feeling.
- Thorough Stage One talk-throughs every day will very quickly start to improve the quality of his work, by focusing his attention on the standard you require.
- Make a rule that every piece of weekend homework must be done in rough first. (Your child will probably not have enough time on school nights to do this consistently.) The final copy will be a piece of work that your child can be proud of.
- Descriptively Praise him for all improvements in attitude as well as work.

f What to do to help your child respect the teachers and the school's rules and policies:

- Never let your child overhear you saying anything even remotely critical about the teachers, homework, school policies,

etc. If you do, you will unintentionally be giving your child tacit permission not to take school seriously.

- Instead, write down your criticisms or complaints as requests, and then address them to the person who could, in theory, do something about your request.
- Descriptively Praise everything you can about the school.

Chapter 10
Improving reading comprehension by improving listening comprehension

Children who "don't read" and "don't listen" are often children who can't listen well. As we saw earlier, they often have an auditory processing weakness. Fortunately, listening is a skill that can be taught and trained. Listening is about paying attention and is a function of the brain, whereas hearing is a function of the ears. When we listen our brains are active:

- First we need to discriminate between similar sounds.
- We choose which sounds to pay attention to and which sounds to tune out as irrelevant. Only then can we comprehend. But as we saw earlier, this auditory figure-ground recognition is often weak in children who are not fulfilling their potential.
- We store the important information in the right order, first in our short-term memory.
- Eventually, with successful repetition, the correct information is transferred to our long-term memory (see Chapter 14, Improving Memory).

If this sequence of events is not happening reliably, both listening comprehension and reading comprehension will remain patchy and immature. If a child is not fully understanding the sentences he hears, how can we possibly hope that he will understand these same sentences when he reads them, even if he is able to decode them accurately?

The auditory weakness is hard-wired into the brain, long before birth. As parents and teachers we will continually have to keep two aims in mind. First, we need to "work around" the child's processing difficulties so that he can access the curriculum without being handicapped by his cognitive weakness.

Second, we need to improve the child's receptive language skills so that he can function more and more independently and maturely. Luckily, the brain is extremely malleable, so the areas of weak functioning can be strengthened considerably. You will notice that some of the following strategies function as crutches: they simplify or slow down the stream of language that is coming into the child's brain. This will give him a better chance of understanding what he hears. Other strategies are designed to strengthen his listening skills. Some of the strategies accomplish both aims.

This chapter explains how parents can:

- motivate children with poor auditory processing to want to listen to parents and teachers, rather than trying to ignore us
- get children into the habit of focusing on what they hear
- teach them to discriminate between similar sounds
- shorten their auditory reaction time (the time it takes for "the penny to drop")
- make it easier for children to understand what they hear and read
- teach them how to judge what is important in what they hear and read
- strengthen their auditory sequencing ability.

As we are helping the child to listen better, we will notice that gradually he is understanding and remembering more of what he reads, enjoying school more, co-operating more quickly and with less fuss, and concentrating for longer periods. Best of all, we will see that he is becoming more competent, more confident, more mature and happier.

The following strategies will help your child learn to listen better:

1 Avoid calling your child's name to get his attention. Children hear their names being called so many times, especially uttered in an irritated tone of voice. They assume something not very pleasant is coming when they hear their name. They may even grow to dislike their name for this reason.

Instead, to get your child's attention, you can:

- Descriptively Praise
- Smile
- Move closer to him and stand, waiting patiently
- Face directly towards him
- Point to him
- Prepare for success by announcing, "I'm about to ask you a question" or, "In a moment I'm going to tell you what to do next". When the child stops what he is doing and looks up at you, smile and take a few moments to appreciate that he has torn himself away from his game to look at you and listen.

2 Make it a firm habit to give and get eye contact before you even begin speaking to your child, whether you are asking, telling or answering. In addition to helping him listen, this first step is basic good manners on our part. We must lead by example.

Weak auditory learners are usually strong visual learners. The information that comes in through their eyes feels very vivid; it grabs their attention. What they are looking at is usually what they will be thinking about. So make a rule *for yourself* that you will only talk to your child while he is looking at you and you are looking at him. If his eyes wander away while you are in mid-flow, stop talking and wait, with a smile. He will soon look back up at you, if only to find out why you suddenly went silent.

Understandably, children try to avoid unpleasant interactions by looking away, sometimes even by walking away. But now that you are learning and practising Descriptive Praise, Reflective Listening and the follow-through techniques, you will see that the natural drive within all children to please their parents is re-surfacing.

3 Keep your voice low. It can be as difficult for this child to understand you when you bellow as when you talk too softly.

4 Keep your voice friendly, calm and enthusiastic. He will not be motivated to listen to a tone that is abrupt, impatient or irritated.

5 Speak more slowly than usual, with longer pauses between sentences and also between the phrases within each sentence. This is how we

automatically speak to young children because we know that they cannot make sense of a long stream of words. The child with poor auditory processing is still at an immature level, so he still needs this from us. Even though this strategy results in better understanding, the child may object at first, calling it "babyish" or protesting "I'm not stupid, you know". Reflectively Listen and persevere, just as you would with a child who needs the "crutch" of glasses for reading. If you stay calm and consistent, he will soon become used to it. And you will notice that he is listening more carefully and understanding more quickly.

6 Make a point of articulating very clearly. This becomes much easier to remember to do when you have made a commitment to speaking more slowly. When we enunciate clearly, the child with auditory discrimination problems is better able to differentiate between words that sound rather similar. In particular, make sure to sound the last consonant in each word.

7 Speak in short, simple sentences. Put each new piece of information into a new sentence. This will help your child to visualise what he hears.

8 Finish your sentences. This seems unnecessary advice because we all assume that we do finish our sentences. Once you start listening to yourself and to others, you will see how common it is for people to start a sentence, not finish their thought, and start a new sentence. This is very confusing and frustrating for children who cannot mentally switch gears quickly.

9 Completely finish each thought before you go on to the next point you want to make. This will cut down on confusion.

10 Before you launch into the details of what you want to tell your child, prepare for success by giving him one or two summary sentences as an introduction. This wakes up the child's brain, alerts him to what he should pay attention to, i.e. what to visualise. Avoid overloading his weak auditory processing with a stream of sentences:

> "Where's your homework diary? I need to see what spellings you've got this week. I hope you copied them down properly.

Last week you got 8 out of 10 right. Do you think you can do even better this week?"

This is too much information coming at him too quickly. It is too great a processing load for a child with an auditory processing weakness. He will feel swamped, even though he is perfectly capable of understanding each sentence, if he is given time to digest each one before the next one comes at him. When he reacts to the river of words by arguing or complaining or changing the subject, parents may assume, incorrectly, that the problem lies with the subject matter or with the teacher or with the school. There may indeed be problems in those areas, but often the underlying problem is that the child cannot translate the words he hears into mental images as quickly as we are talking.

It is more helpful to introduce the topic very simply, by saying something like this: "Now it's time to practise your spellings". Then stop talking and wait for a response. It may take him longer than you wish it would to register what you just said. The child may begin searching for his spelling list, in which case you can Descriptively Praise: "You're getting started even before I told you to. That's self-reliance (or responsibility, or courage, etc.)." Or the child may complain or argue. That is your cue to Reflectively Listen: "You probably wish you were a naturally good speller!" or "Maybe you're worried that you'll make lots of mistakes and I'll get annoyed". Then wait for him to respond.

11 There may be many occasions during the talk-through stage of the daily homework session, as well as at other times, when you will feel tempted to repeat yourself, for example if he was not listening the first time you said something or if he seems confused or if he impulsively makes the same mistake again and again.

Don't repeat yourself! If you do, his brain will not get the message that he needs to listen. Here is what to do instead:

- Before you start speaking, wait and make sure that he is looking at you and not fiddling with anything. To make it as easy as possible for your child to pay attention, you will need to take responsibility for removing all possible distractions.

- If he looks away or starts fiddling while you are talking, pause and wait for his attention.
- Keep explanations short. After two sentences, you have probably lost his attention.
- Keep him focused by pausing after every two or three sentences and asking him to tell you what you just said. Do not move on to your next point until he can tell you in his own words. That is how you can be certain that he has not only heard but understood. If all he has to do is parrot back what you said, you cannot gauge how thoroughly he understands.

12 Get into the habit of repeating and emphasising key words when you are explaining. The repetitions will help his brain sort the incoming information more efficiently.

13 Challenge yourself to use more concrete and more vivid vocabulary, which will help your child construct a clearer mental picture.

14 Help your child increase the number of words and ideas he understands. One way to achieve this is by using an unfamiliar synonym, explaining what it means and then immediately asking the child to tell you the meaning. Ask him several times, and each time phrase your question slightly differently. For example, you could say,

> "I see that all your dictation sentences this week have to do with motion. Motion means moving. Motion means......? Another way to say motion is....? We can say moving or we can say....?"

15 Do not take it for granted that your child understands the specialised terminology of his school subjects. It is entirely possibly for a child to correctly answer multiple-choice tests and short-answer exams without quite knowing what he is reading about. Teachers do discuss definitions, but rarely spend as much time reinforcing them as children with school problems need. So it will be your job to make sure he thoroughly understands the vocabulary of each subject.

Always define new vocabulary using very familiar vocabulary. You will notice that the more comfortable he is with the language of a subject, the more interested and engaged he will be. He will be able to better understand what he hears and reads.

16 Whenever your child asks a question, instead of immediately answering, first have him take a sensible guess. Be prepared to wait and insist. When he guesses, find something to Descriptively Praise. Routinely requiring him to answer his own questions will gradually:

- Sharpen his brain's ability to retrieve information that has been stored in his memory.
- Give him practice at working things out for himself, a skill he will certainly need when you are not around, for example at school, with his peers and later in a job.
- Give him experiences of competence and self-reliance; these are the keys to confidence and self-esteem.
- Show him that he can get positive attention for being sensible, so he will be less and less tempted to get attention by asking unnecessary or irrelevant questions.

17 Information that enters the brain via two senses will be stored more securely, so whenever you are demonstrating how to do something, also use words to explain. And when you are explaining, whenever possible also demonstrate.

18 Harness your child's visual strengths to shore up his auditory weakness. As you and he speak about homework (or about anything he is not particularly interested in or might forget) jot down a list of the points or the steps in a procedure. Draw a diagram to illustrate something he is confused about. Gradually build up a collection of mini-posters to act as visual aids. For example, you can make lists of:

- Mathematics:
  - Words and phrases that tell him that he has to "take away", such as "subtract, remaining, less than, what is left, minus, find the difference etc.".
  - The steps involved in solving a long multiplication sum. (If your child is having difficulty remembering a

procedure, find out from the school how it is being taught.)

- Essay-Writing:
    - More expressive words to use instead of *nice* or *fun* or *great* when writing a story, for example, *exciting, enjoyable, satisfying, useful, impressive.*
    - Steps for writing an essay.
- Spelling:
    - Sight words that cannot be spelled correctly simply by sounding them out because they contain a silent letter, such as *comb, fasten, guess, bridge.*
    - Words that are spelled the same but have more than one meaning, for example, *hound, ball, train, habit, bear.*
- History: The names of famous people he has come across in his lessons, his reading or in conversation, and what they are famous for, e.g.:

Richard Branson	Herod
Hilary Clinton	Joan of Arc
Marie Curie	Martin Luther King
Queen Elizabeth I	Florence Nightingale
Guy Fawkes	Pocahontas
Mahatma Gandhi	St George
Henry VIII	Mother Theresa

- Foreign Language:
    - French verbs that end in "er"
    - Idioms
- Reading Comprehension: Unfamiliar phrases and idiomatic expressions that he has come across in his reading and what they mean, for example:
    - Metaphors
        Bull in a china shop
        Bright-eyed and bushy-tailed
        Broken-hearted
        Two-faced
        Having several strings to one's bow

- Similes

>   Cool as a cucumber
>   Looked like he was dragged through a hedge
>   backwards
>   Happy as a sand boy
>   Clean as a whistle
>   Mad as a hatter

- Proverbs

>   Don't burn your bridges before you cross them
>   If the shoe fits, wear it
>   Too many cooks spoil the broth
>   Many a true word is spoken in jest
>   Old dogs can't learn new tricks

- Old-fashioned or literary expressions, such as *nook and cranny, hue and cry, aid and abet.*

19 Make a game of saying a sentence and having your child pick out a particular part of speech, e.g. nouns. With time, this will help him understand the relationships among words within a sentence.

20 Make a game of saying a sentence that includes a grammatical mistake or a contradiction or an inaccuracy. Then have your child identify the mistake and say the sentence correctly. This trains him to pay more careful attention to the flow of words that swirl around him. Take turns so that your child gets practice at composing the incorrect sentences, as this will also help him become aware of correct usage. Examples might be:

- Incorrect grammar:
  - "He done his homework."
  - "She teached me how to play the guitar."
- Contradictions:
  - "He hated broccoli so he asked for a second helping."
  - "He walked across the road carefully, with his eyes closed."
- Inaccuracies:
  - "She ate the banana and spat out the seeds."

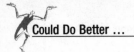

– "For the Easter assembly, the class rehearsed their
    Nativity play."

Everything that helps a child understand more fully what he hears and
reads will also help him to make himself understood when he speaks and
in his writing. So this chapter and the next (which focuses on speaking
and writing) should be read together and implemented at the same time.

Chapter 11

Learning to love reading:
A one-year plan for parents

A year's commitment may seem like a very long time, but we must remember that children and teenagers who "don't read enough" or who "don't read much" are not simply children who don't want to read. Usually they have experienced that they are not good at reading, and they believe that reading will never hold pleasure for them. Often they feel embarrassed and guilty about not being "readers". So we can see that not being a reader is not just the absence of a good habit. It is the presence of a negative habit. That negative habit, the habit of not reading, and the subtle distress accompanying it, has been in the making, reinforced daily by avoidance, for many years. It can take a long time to dissolve.

The most important thing for parents to remember is:

This programme works if *you* work it.

And the rewards are great. Besides opening up to your child the riches of learning, adventure and insight that reading brings, you will find that participating in this programme together for a year will strengthen and deepen the bond of love and understanding between you and your child. It will stand you in very good stead during the difficult times. You and your child will be allies, rather than adversaries.

Slavish adherence to this programme (and this programme requires nothing less) will result in a love of reading. I have never seen it fail in over thirty years of teaching and working with parents. You will notice that most of my advice is just plain common sense; there are no gimmicks or tricks. But the key is consistency. As with everything else in life, it works only if you work.

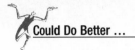

Preparing yourself and disciplining yourself: The parents' job

a. Set aside time

Six days a week, including holidays, set aside half an hour a day with your
child and an additional ten minutes preparation and evaluation time by
yourself. This is the most important step because without the automatic
expectation (on your part as well as the child's) that this half-hour will
really happen, come what may, the initial determination and enthusiasm
will fizzle out after a few weeks, under the pressure of other, more
pressing time commitments.

On Saturdays and holidays do it early in the day, before the day's
demands grab each of you and pull you off in opposite directions.

b. Parents are in charge

Assume that you, the parent, are totally in charge of making this
programme work. You are the one who makes sure that you both sit
down together for a half-hour every day. Never nag about it. Never expect
him to take the initiative. He will, eventually, be eager for this half-hour,
but it will probably take longer than you think it will. He, like all non-
lovers of reading, especially adolescents, has built up a very strong
unconscious defence system against something that seems very distasteful
and boring to him. His defences will not melt away in a few days or even
a few months. They must be whittled away gradually, lovingly, almost
imperceptibly.

c. Plan in advance

Plan in advance when you will fit this sacred and inviolate half-hour into
your day. Right after supper is often best on weekdays, but many parents
have reported success with right after breakfast. It means getting up
earlier, but it makes a very positive and calming start to the day.

d. Be prepared for your child's reaction

Even though your child may be very eager, in theory, to improve his
reading skills and to overcome his ingrained distaste of reading, it is really

too much to expect him to enjoy and look forward with delight to the process for quite a long time. None of us relishes the effort it requires to transform bad habits into good ones, no matter how thrilled we are sure we would be with the results of our efforts.

e. Make-up sessions

If, for any reason, you absolutely must skip a day, double up the day *before*, not the day after. And double up by having two separate half-hours (not one long session of an hour, which would feel interminable). If you discipline yourself to do all make-up sessions before, rather than after, the day you have to miss, you will feel virtuous and ahead-of-the-game, rather than guilty and dreading it. Your child needs this discipline, and you may also!

The first six months

A Planning: The parent's job

And now for the basic daily format, which is very simple:

- 15 minutes of reading together; and
- 15 minutes of "digestion" together.

Any child or teenager can handle 15 minutes of reading if he knows that is all he will be expected to do and if the second part of the half-hour is kept lively and interesting and non-critical, which is the parents' job.

Choose short passages from books, articles, short stories, poetry, scenes from plays, etc. that you think might appeal to your child. Each selection must feel complete within the 15 minutes, so that you both feel that you have read something that you can really get your teeth into and understand.

Keep an eye and ear out for what might interest him. Keep an ongoing list of possible choices. You keep the list, not your child. Don't worry about whether any one selection is just right or not. Even if it turns out to be a bad choice, carry on reading for the full 15 minutes. Your child

needs to experience that he can survive 15 minutes of a topic or literary style that does not instantly appeal to him. Day by day, through noticing his reactions to the passages you select, you will both be learning more about what makes your child tick.

Choose reading material that can be completed over one to five sessions, rather than whole books. One of our aims is to introduce the young person to the joys of many different types of material. Also, we need to remember that many non-readers are convinced it would require a super-human effort for them to slog their way through a book to the bitter end. We do not want to put the child off by expecting him to do what he is convinced he will not enjoy doing. We must build up to it in very small, almost painless steps.

Show enthusiasm for whatever kind of reading material he suggests or brings to you, even comics or the instruction manual for a computer game. There is something positive and useful in almost every experience. Your job is to find it, appreciate it, and share it with him. This is not the time for criticism, no matter how objective or well-meaning.

B What the parent and child will be doing during the daily half-hour session

First 15 minutes:

Take turns reading aloud, *alternating sentences, not paragraphs or pages.* Often, even a short paragraph is too large a chunk because the child's mind can easily drift away to other thoughts when it is your turn to read aloud. Many non-readers feel that they are unable to concentrate on what they are reading. Actually, they just have not yet learned *how* to concentrate on what they are reading. We will lead them, by small steps, to see that, without even realising it, they have been paying attention to and absorbing what they are reading.

Reading aloud is a very different skill from reading silently. Many children, even many teenagers, have not practised reading aloud regularly enough to achieve fluency and natural expression. Nervousness is also a contributing factor to lack of fluency. So, to set your child at ease, *never* criticise how he reads. Descriptively Praise whenever possible.

A non-fluent reader has often developed the habit of rushing or stumbling through the task in a monotone, barely paying attention to the meaning, inserting words that are not really there and leaving out or slightly altering the words that are on the page.

The most effective and the quickest way to help children improve their oral reading skills is to make a firm rule for both of you that each sentence must be read smoothly and completely correctly before the other person can begin reading the next sentence. So whenever one of you makes even a slight mistake, that person will need to read that whole sentence again from its beginning, rather than simply correctly repeating the words or phrase where the problem was. Lead by example; be very willing to say, "I didn't quite pronounce that properly, so I'll start my sentence all over again".

No one wants to read the same sentence over and over again. So this rule, if rigorously enforced, will quickly establish new habits: slowing down, scanning ahead a bit, thinking about meaning as he reads, reading with more expression.

Sometimes a child will make a mistake in reading and not even realise it. Often, all you need to do is pause; don't begin reading your sentence yet. This silently signals to your child that there was a problem in his sentence, and it avoids parental criticism and annoyance. At this point the child will usually check over his sentence and notice for himself where his mistake was. If he cannot see it, give him a clue, but whenever possible avoid telling him directly. Once again, we want the child's brain to do the work.

If he makes the same kind of mistake again and again, make sure you notice every time he does it correctly (or even slightly better) and Descriptively Praise that. Consciously or unconsciously, he will absorb this message and will strive to repeat the satisfying experience of being appreciated. Remember to make the praise very specific so that he knows exactly what it is he is aiming for.

End the period of reading aloud together after *exactly* 15 minutes. Do not extend the time, no matter how interested either of you may be. If you break this rule, your child will not be able to trust you to keep your word. Use a

timer, if necessary, to convince your child that you are not trying to sneak in extra minutes. Stop in mid-sentence as soon as the timer goes off, so that he learns to trust that 15 minutes of reading really means only 15 minutes.

Second 15 minutes:

Next comes digestion. This can take many forms, but you must avoid simply talking about what you have just been reading together. General discussion about a topic can often deteriorate into the parent talking and the child listening (or not listening), or the parent asking questions and the child answering in mono-syllables. There is just too much pressure on the child to come up with articulate and profound comments.

To avoid the danger of simply talking about the reading, discipline yourself to stick to the exercises listed below (plus others you will generate yourselves). These exercises will probably stimulate more thought and interest than just talking about what you have read. You will soon start to notice that spontaneous discussion of the passages will occur at other times of the day. But let it always come from the child. If, outside of the half-hour reading time, you want to refer to the reading material or to a topic you have read about together, you may occasionally drop very tiny pebbles into the pond to see what ripples they create, but you must be prepared to let them sink without a trace if your child does not respond.

I have listed here a number of possible exercises to stimulate thinking (perception, comprehension, interpretation, logic, etc.) and language skills. Keep a list of additional exercises that you or he think of (or hear or read about). Next to each exercise jot down the date you did it and a word or two about whether it was successful or not, why or how. This will ensure that you do not do any one exercise more often than once a week. We are striving for freshness and a variety of experiences.

Exercises:

These will always to be done by the parent and the child together. We can assume that a reluctant child will need encouragement through Descriptive Praise and Reflective Listening. In addition, the child will be less anxious if the parent demonstrates how to do the exercise by taking the first turn.

a Each of you pretends to be a character from the passage and hold a conversation, trying to stay in character. Then switch roles.

b One of you pretends to be a character, or the author, and be interviewed by the other. Then switch roles.

c Together, imagine that you are one of the characters or the author. Invent a background for him or her (childhood, important memories, passions, fears, etc.).

d Together, invent an alternative ending. Try for: sad, happy, unlikely, realistic, funny, gruesome, etc.

e Each of you predict what might happen next and explain why you think that could happen.

f Take turns paraphrasing the passage using language that a 7 year old child would understand.

g Take turns paraphrasing the passage using teenage slang.

h Act out something from the reading.

i Take turns asking interesting questions about the passage for the other to answer.

j Take turns imagining what led up to the events of the passage.

k Take turns mentioning all the little things you like and dislike about the passage. Justify your opinions.

l Choose one part of speech, (nouns, adjectives, verbs, adverbs, etc) and take turns naming all the words that fall into that category. See if you can come up with synonyms (words that mean the same) for each.

m Now try the above exercise with antonyms (words with opposite meanings).

n Give each other a spelling quiz using words from the passage.

o Together, decide which words and phrases the author uses to build up the atmosphere or tone of the passage.

p Look for words, phrases or sentences that you both think could be altered to convey the author's meaning more clearly.

q Give each other a comprehension quiz.

r Take turns expressing an opinion on the passage, and your reasons for it, as if you were:

a history teacher

a ballerina

a waitress

a mathematical genius

a musician

a horse trainer

an actress

a single mother of five children

a football player

a homeless person

etc. etc.

Notice how your perceptions and concerns change depending on the occupation and life circumstances of the person you pretend to be.

s   Together, imagine what kind of person the author might have been to have written the piece. Focus on either content or style.

t   Take turns making speeches declaiming the opposite of what you see as the author's message. Be as convincing as possible.

Now that you see the sorts of exercises that enhance comprehension and enjoyment, you and your child will be able to make up other exercises. You can decide together which exercise you will do each day, as long as no more than one minute is spent on reaching the decision. Indecision saps commitment and enthusiasm. If you can't agree together, then you, the parent, should decide quickly. (Prepare for success by telling your child beforehand that this is the policy.) Once you have decided on the exercise, spend the whole 15 minutes on that one exercise. If it does not seem to be going well, modify it, but do not scrap it. We want to teach and reinforce willingness and perseverance.

Even if the exercise is going well and you are tempted to go over the 15 minute limit – DON'T! It is always better, just as in show business, to "leave 'em wanting more".

Always end the session on an up note of success: a hug, Descriptive Praise and humour.

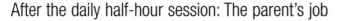

After the daily half-hour session: The parent's job

Between the end of one day's session and the beginning of the next, your job is to spend *no more than 10 minutes* on the following:

- Record which passage was read.
- Record which exercise you did together.
- Jot down how it went, what you learned from it, what to do again or what to do differently, etc.
- Choose the next day's passage (from your list of possible choices).

Helping your child move through his uncomfortable emotions

Stay willing to Reflectively Listen to the child's uncomfortable feelings about: this programme, reading, himself in relation to reading, himself in general, textbooks, school, life, anything! Acknowledge the sincerity and seriousness of his feelings and opinions.

Reflective Listening shows him that you take his feelings seriously enough to really try and hear what he is going through, rather than to interrupt immediately with your adult version of reality. As parents, we have to really stop everything for a few minutes and put ourselves in our child's shoes to see his life through his eyes. If the feeling we reflect back to him is not accurate, the child may or may not correct us. It is helpful to keep listening and reflecting back what we imagine the child is feeling until he lets us know, through words or actions, that he feels understood or appreciated. Our willingness to listen attentively, without arguing, is often all the child needs.

But make sure to keep these discussions out of the precious half-hour of reading and digesting, or else the time can be eroded all too easily. Complaining can also become a manipulative device on the child's part. At other times of the day (but not at bedtime) be ready, when you can make the time, to drop everything and listen. Often comment is unnecessary and unwelcome, and all that may be needed is a smile or a hug or a word of empathy.

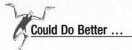

The second six months

After six months of following this programme to the letter, you then move on to the second phase of the programme for the next six months. This is exactly the same plan but, instead of a half-hour every day, it is one hour four times a week. We want to build up the child's stamina, so that he can read for longer and longer periods without tiring. The format is exactly the same except:

- A half-hour of reading and a half-hour of "digestion".
- After five minutes of reading aloud, alternating sentences, you may both do the rest of the day's reading silently. (This requires two copies of the text.)
- You may tackle whole books, but only books that the child is absolutely keen to read – no subtle suggestions, please.
- The exercises may include writing, but only if your child is completely comfortable with writing. Absolutely no "constructive criticism" of handwriting, spelling or punctuation is allowed!

By the end of one year, things will be *very different*. Your children or teenager will enjoy reading, he will be willing to read widely, and you and he will be closer. You and your child can then decide together whether you will carry on with the programme, modify it, or drop it altogether. Many families choose to carry on but cut back to once or twice a week. Some families have chosen to keep those four hours a week sacred but to substitute other shared activities in the place of reading and digestion. Some families have done a combination of the two.

Chapter 12

Improving writing skills by improving speaking skills

Children need to be taught how to make themselves easily understood when they are talking before we can ever expect them to make themselves understood in their writing. Parents can most easily teach and train this skill because they are guiding the child's communication every day. The ability to make oneself understood starts with thinking clearly. Then the clear thoughts need to be phrased in clear language. Let us look at clear thinking first. There are several key thinking skills that a child must master in order to communicate clearly.

He needs to realise that the listener or reader does not automatically know what he knows. This may sound obvious, but a young child does not understand this, so he will announce, "James broke it" and then be surprised when the adult asks who James is or what got broken. This can continue to be a problem for an older child who is relatively immature for his age, or a child with subtle specific learning difficulties. This child understands, in theory, that a listener does not necessarily know what he knows, but he easily forgets this important fact, particularly when he is excited or upset. So what he says often does not quite make sense. The listener or reader has to supply or clarify the missing information. This can exasperate his teachers and make his peers think him odd or babyish.

Another thinking skill which is essential to clear communication is understanding what the listener or reader wants to know. This falls in the category of "figure-ground recognition", discussed in Chapter 4.

The child also needs to know how to evaluate whether the listener has understood what the child just said. Ordinarily in conversations we rely on the listener's facial expressions and verbal responses to let us know if we need to explain further. But a child can easily miss or misinterpret these signs, particularly if he is anxious, absorbed in the details of what

he is saying, or simply immature. And of course when the child is writing, the reader is not generally present to give feedback.

A child with subtle specific learning difficulties has a brain which is capable of learning the skills of thinking clearly and expressing himself clearly. But his brain will need to he taught these skills, whereas another child, without these cognitive weaknesses, will automatically develop these skills as he matures, without needing targeted training. Here are some useful strategies that will help your child become a more successful communicator, both in speaking and in writing:

- Children with poor expressive language often feel embarrassed and anxious when they are called on to explain something. They register the subtle or not-so-subtle signs of annoyance, or possibly even ridicule, on the faces of the listeners. They may feel put on the spot even if parents and teachers are not impatient or judgmental. They may become hesitant, unwilling to volunteer information. Or they may adopt the opposite tack and ramble aimlessly, hoping that by luck they will finally answer the question correctly and satisfy their questioner. Whenever possible, give this child a bit of advance notice that you are about to ask him a question. You might say:

  > "Pretty soon I will ask you to tell me three things you can remember about your history lesson."
  > "In a minute I will ask you to explain how to do these sums."

  The extra bit of thinking time you are building in will significantly reduce his anxiety and result in less confused and more fluent responses.

- Asking short questions will help your child to marshal his thoughts. It is helpful to ask several short questions about a topic or event and get several short answers, rather than asking a long question that has several parts and expecting a long answer. For each short question the child will only need to retrieve a small amount of information and put it into the

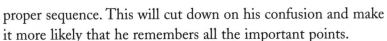

proper sequence. This will cut down on his confusion and make it more likely that he remembers all the important points.

- Ask your child many questions every day, during the homework sessions and whenever you are in the same room together, in the car, at mealtimes, while waiting in a queue, etc. This will give him vital practise at retrieving information from his memory storage, selecting the relevant bits of information and choosing the words that will get that information across to you, the listener. Many children who are not achieving their potential at school have poor attention to detail and therefore also poor recall of details. One way to help these children develop the habit of paying closer attention to what they see and hear is to hold them accountable by asking them questions that require them to notice what is going on around them. Another common area of difficulty for atypical learners is the understanding of cause and effect, in particular understanding what motivates people to respond in various ways. So we also need to ask questions that give them practice at focusing on and examining and exploring these aspects. For example:

  - In the car: "What street are we in?"
  - At the supermarket: "Tell me the names of four salad vegetables you can see".
  - In the dentist's waiting room: "What does that sign remind everyone to do?" and "What would happen if people forgot to do that?"
  - When reading to him: "Who wrote this book?", "Why did the boy keep looking out of the window?" and "What do you think will happen next?"

- When you ask a question, be prepared to wait for a delayed response that is due to slow reaction time.

- When you ask a question, do not accept the response of "I don't know". Staying friendly and calm, insist that the child take a sensible guess, and be willing to wait as long as it takes. A child is always capable of guessing. Training a child not to give up does wonders for his self-reliance and self-confidence. Even if

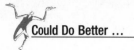

your child's guess is incorrect, find something to Descriptively Praise, for example his courage in being willing to take a guess.

- Require your child to answer your questions in full sentences. This may not be easy for him to do at first. But it has several benefits:

  - This requirement makes the child slow down and think about what he is going to say, rather than blurt it out impulsively.
  - All the important information will be stored together in his long-term memory, rather than in isolated chunks. For example, you may ask, "What is 4 times 6?" Even if the child correctly replies "24", all that will be stored in his memory is "24". This results in the familiar scenario where children know that 24, 48, 49 etc. are multiplication answers but have no clue which table they are in. So when you ask, "What is 4 times 6?" have your child answer "4 times 6 is 24". That way the brain will store the question and the answer together, as one piece of information. Also, storing a sequence of words will greatly help written expression.

- Whenever your child makes a mistake with language, have him repeat the whole sentence correctly. So if he tells you, "And then Harry *brang* the book to my desk", don't just say, "It's not *brang*, it's *brought*". Don't just ask "And then Harry what?" and be satisfied if he answers "*brought*". Have him repeat the whole sentence correctly. He may resist this new practice at first because it is uncomfortable to face one's mistakes. Persevere. This technique results in storage in the long-term memory of the correct vocabulary or sentence construction. To take some of the sting out of this for the child, be generous about admitting your own language mistakes. You can say, "Oops, I said that wrong, so I'm going to start my sentence all over again, so that it really makes sense".

- When something that your child says does not quite make sense, do not supply the missing information for him. When he tells you, "I saw Thomas", don't say, "Do you mean Thomas the Tank Engine? You watched Thomas the Tank Engine on TV today?" In that example, the parent's brain is doing the job of clarifying. Instead, we need to make the child's brain do the work. Also, don't simply ask him what he is talking about, which can make an inarticulate child even more tongue-tied. First say what you understand, and then what you do not understand. You might say, "I know Thomas is a boy's name, so I'm guessing you saw a boy called Thomas today. Or was it a man?" When we ask the child to choose between two or more possible meanings, this is called *clarification by contrast*. Presenting the child with a limited number of possibilities to choose from makes the task of explaining much less daunting for him. And it models for him how people clarify things that are confusing. If you are willing to use this clarification technique several times every day, over time your child will start to predict and pre-empt these questions by supplying the necessary information before you have to ask for it.

- Whenever you are reading to your child or telling him a story, pause every few sentences and have your child:

  - repeat a phrase or sentence verbatim
  - restate in his own words what just happened
  - give a synonym or definition for a word or phrase
  - answer a "why" question
  - make up a question for you to answer

Of course, he needs to speak in complete sentences.

- Make a frequent habit of elaborating and expanding on what your child says. This models more mature communication. For example, if he says, "The giraffes are big", you can extend his understanding and vocabulary by saying, "Yes, giraffes are very tall. They have long, long, long legs and a long, long neck. So they're very tall". Then you can immediately reinforce this concept and start cementing it in his memory: "Giraffes are very…?" "That's right, they're tall. Giraffes have very long…?" "Yes, their necks are long, and their legs are long".

- Read to your child every day, long past the age when he is capable of reading to himself. Children need to continually hear more mature vocabulary and sentence construction than they are exposed to in the books they might choose to read to themselves. If your child is extremely restless and fidgety, he may find sitting still and listening to you read "boring". So read to him while he is playing with his blocks or Lego™. In addition to bedtimes, mealtimes present another ideal opportunity to read to children.

- To help a child expand his vocabulary so that he can convey more precise shades of meaning, play a game in which you both look carefully at an object, either in real life, in your imaginations or in a picture. Together you take turns coming up with as many adjectives as possible to describe that noun. For example, for a flower, you and your child might think of: "yellow, white, leafy, soft, light, pretty, small, delicate, sweet-smelling, fluffy, shiny, wet, poisonous", etc.

- Help children become comfortable with generating ideas and composing sentences by practising "spoken word mini-essays". To make it more like a game and to model how to do it, the parent and child should alternate turns (with the parent always being willing to go first, if the child is at all reluctant or resistant). Each of you chooses a topic that you are familiar with and then says five to ten sentences about this topic, starting with an introductory sentence that sets the scene and ending with a conclusion that summarises the mini-essay. As always, find a lot to Descriptively Praise. As your child gradually becomes more skilled, you can require more diverse topics, more mature development of ideas, more precise vocabulary, and more interesting sentence construction. This exercise enables your child to practise many important aspects of writing without the slog of having to control his pencil and without the worrying distractions of spelling and punctuation. Therefore, it goes quickly and is relatively painless. And it results in rapid, solid improvements in clear communication and confidence.

As you practise the above suggestions, you or your child will probably like some of them better than others. Do not skimp on the ones that are less appealing or are harder work. Feel free to temporarily simplify any that are too great a challenge for your child, but do them all. You will be giving your child the priceless gift of clearer communication, improved school success skills and greater confidence in himself.

Chapter 13
Proof-reading and improving written work

As adults, we know that our first attempt at anything is rarely our very best effort. When writing anything important, (e.g., a C.V., a report for work, a letter), we always proof-read and improve our first draft, often rewriting it several times. Children need to learn this process and get into the habit of proof-reading. Some will fall into this habit quite easily, whilst others, usually the impulsive, impatient ones will resist, either actively or passively. They manage to defeat the best efforts of parents and teachers to motivate and encourage them to pay attention to the details that need improving.

It takes these children a long time to learn how to proof-read effectively, and even after they know how, they may do it sketchily. It seems as if they just can't be bothered to slow down and pay attention to details. Of course, this affects their marks at school, and even, over time, their self-esteem because they are reprimanded so frequently. They come to see themselves as lazy or stupid. As we saw in Section II, this is far from the truth. These are often children with subtle specific learning difficulties, eg. weak visual figure-ground recognition, for whom proof-reading is genuinely difficult.

These children *can* be trained to proof-read, edit and improve their written work. The responsibility for this training will usually fall on parents because teachers rarely have the time. Parents need to view this training as an ongoing project. It takes time and determination.

There are two ways to teach and train proof-reading and editing skills:

- within the context of the child's homework
- in isolation, e.g. activities and games designed to target specific micro-skills.

Parents will need to keep in mind some general principles that govern the teaching and training of proof-reading.

1 Do not assume that the child knows how to proof-read accurately but is being careless or "lazy". It is highly unlikely that he has mastered the micro-skills necessary for proof-reading, editing and improving his written work.

- He may not be paying careful attention in class when the teacher discusses proof-reading
- Some pupils have not been taught proof-reading techniques, other than hearing their teachers saying occasionally, "Check your work."
- And yet others may have been taught how to proof-read well enough to be able to tell you all about what to do, but they rush to get the work over and done with and omit or skim over the proof-reading stage.
- Some children diligently read over their work, but do not notice their mistakes. They "see" what they expect to see.

2 For two important reasons, the daily homework talk-through is the very first step in teaching and training proof-reading. Talk-throughs teach and train the child to monitor his work as he is producing it. And because talk-throughs always result in a higher standard of homework, the child is then much more willing, during Stage Three, to tackle the smaller number of errors.

3 In order to be able to proof-read effectively, a child or young person needs to have developed the following skills, habits and attitudes:

- pride in his work, so that he wants to improve it
- sufficient self-confidence to know that he is not a failure, even when he makes mistakes
- the habit of attention to detail
- knowledge of what the teacher will be looking for
- knowledge of what is correct or acceptable and what is not.

4 The child needs to be taught the micro-skills necessary for proof-reading and editing before you can even begin to hope that any proof-reading advice you give will be understood, retained and used.

- Teach (and revise frequently) the use of a spelling dictionary or spell checker.
- Choose a user-friendly dictionary for checking meanings.
- Teach the use of a thesaurus for enriching vocabulary.
- Have the child, under guidance, refer to a simple grammar book for rules governing punctuation.
- Frequently point out formal versus informal sentence construction so that your child learns that what is acceptable in speech is often not acceptable in writing.
- When you are talking with your child, model and help him practise clear versus vague sentence construction.
- Teach attention to detail in everything, not just homework.

As your child learns these micro-skills, you will notice that teaching proof-reading is no longer frustrating; in fact, it can even be exciting and rewarding.

5   We need to distinguish between two very different activities:

- Teaching and training the techniques and strategies necessary for proof-reading
- Getting the child's homework corrected before he hands it in to the school. This should not be our goal. If it is, we may be tempted to tell him how to improve his work rather than taking the time necessary to help him discover for himself what needs to be corrected and why and how. Sometimes we do this because we feel "the work must get done." This is a fallacy! Learning takes as long as it takes. All children are different, so we cannot and must not undertake to make sure that they finish a certain amount of work by 7pm or that they reach a certain standard by the end of the term. Our job as parents is to teach and train the important skills, concepts, attitudes, habits and values. We cannot accurately predict how long this will take for each child.

6   You can expect the resistant child to argue, complain, negotiate or try to distract you:

"What's wrong with that?"

"My teacher doesn't mind if I do it like that." (Don't take the child's word for it!)

"That's the way I always do it."

"That's stupid!"

"I can't."

"It doesn't matter."

"Why do I have to?"

"That's how we do it at school." (Possibly, but don't assume the teacher is happy with it.)

"But that's right."

"It's because I'm dyslexic."

"That's what I meant to do."

"I know how to do that already."

"Can I have a break?"

"This is boring."

"You're the strictest dad in the whole world."

"I'm no good at English."

"Do we have to talk about it? Can't I just do it?"

Don't try to reason with a child who is being unreasonable; it usually makes the child even more stubborn. You will probably need to do plenty of Reflective Listening because children who are not fulfilling their potential often have very negative feelings about their work in general and about proof-reading in particular. This is because it focuses on their weaknesses, and no one enjoys that! Reflective Listening achieves several purposes. It:

- Shows the child that the parent cares and is trying to understand how he feels.
- Gives the child a vocabulary for identifying his negative feelings, which is the first step towards problem-solving.
- Gives the child an arena for expressing negative feelings verbally, so that he does not need to express them through inappropriate behaviour, resistance, complaining, etc.
- Often gives the parent useful information about what the child feels, wants, needs, believes, knows, etc.

So stay calm and cheerful, finding something to empathise with in each complaint.

7 Use humour as a basic tool to keep the atmosphere light. But avoid sarcasm, which can sting.

8 Whenever you can, model the desired proof-reading behaviour. Let the child see you proof-reading your own work, even if it is just a sentence or two that you have written. Muse aloud to show what the thought processes involved are. For example, you could say,

- "Hmmm, I wonder if I spelt that right. I'll look it up to make sure."
- "Should that be a colon or a semi-colon? Actually, maybe it would sound better if I made those into two separate sentences. Now, how does that sound? Yes, much better".
- "I wrote so fast that my handwriting got messy. I had better write this list over again."
- "I'm not sure exactly what that word means. I'll get the dictionary and find out."

Of course, this takes time, but it will pay off sooner than you think.

9 Whenever a child notices an error that you have missed, be delighted. Give Descriptive Praise that focuses on the child's attention to detail and proof-reading skills.

10 Never simply launch into an explanation of how to correct or improve your child's work because:

- Many children have heard it all before.
- Often there is only a fuzzy understanding of the terminology we are using or of basic concepts we are taking for granted.
- When we explain anything to children before finding out what they already know and can do, we risk underestimating and possibly insulting them (and wasting our time and theirs). Or we may unwittingly pitch our explanations over their heads, which leads to even more confusion, resentment and discouragement.

10 Do not fall into the trap of answering questions that the child could figure out or look up for himself. He may need help with this process,

and it will certainly be slower than if you simply explain, but he will learn and remember much more if his brain does the work.

How to teach and train proof-reading:

1 Regularly discuss with your child how even the greatest authors do not expect to be able to produce perfect work the first time. There is absolutely no shame attached to having to proof-read your work.

2 Talk often with your child about how writing (especially if it is creative writing) and proof-reading are different skills which each use a different part of the brain. Children are often fascinated by how their bodies and minds work.

3 Separate in time the writing stage from the proof-reading stage. When possible, wait until the next day before coming back to the work. If that is not possible, a short break is better than none. It allows the child's brain to shift function.

4 Whenever there is enough time, require each piece of homework to be done in rough first (even worksheets). (The exception to this would be exam practice, where the writing is done under exam-type conditions.) Starting with a rough draft enables your child to relax and focus on getting his ideas down, without being hampered by the need to keep in his working memory the details of punctuation, capital letters, spelling and handwriting. You may be concerned that writing both a rough and a final copy would take too much time. Interestingly, it usually saves time. Children soon come to enjoy writing their rough draft, once they realise they are temporarily freed from the drudgery and anxiety of attention to detail. Even die-hard avoiders of writing waste less time getting started and often whiz through the rough draft. Eventually a rough draft will not always be necessary because your child will learn to proof-read his writing *as he writes*, resulting in a better and better standard of work.

5 Have the child skip alternate lines on all rough work. This leaves plenty of space for corrections, additions etc.

6 Have the child use a pencil for all rough work. Encourage rubbing out. Have the child rub out *completely* so that no marks remain.

7 Once the rough draft is completed, put lots of time and attention into finding and appreciating all the good things in the homework. Help him to see and say what he has done right. Be very specific in your Descriptive Praise. For example:

- "You have correctly used some very technical words in this essay. Even someone with no knowledge of the topic, like me, can understand."
- "You have put a capital letter for *every single* proper noun; now I can easily tell who is who."
- "You have really mastered the use of full stops. There is not a single run-on sentence in this essay!"

8 With the child, generate a checklist of all of the aspects of the work that you could examine. Do this each time your child is about to proof-read and edit a new piece of work, rather than referring to a previous checklist, so that the child starts to memorise and internalise the points.

9 Then discuss which aspects your child will proof-read and in which order. Let the ideas come from the child. Be willing to wait for the child's contributions! Find something to praise or agree with in each idea the child offers. Avoid "But…". Keep a list of the useful points generated in this discussion.

10 To make the corrections easier for the child to see when he comes to write out his final copy, the child and parent should use a coloured pen for marking. Avoid red, which often has negative associations.

11 Even when you are drawing the child's attention to an error, practise making your point through Descriptive Praise. For example, you could say:

- "You've written seven sentences here, and five of them start with a capital letter. You've put capitals at the beginning of almost all of your sentences."

- "Your handwriting is so much easier to read now that you are keeping most of the letters on the line."
- "You've got all the right letters here, but they are not yet in the right order."

This motivates the child to find, and to improve, his mistakes.

12 *Make the child's brain do the work.* Have the child tell you what the correction should be and why. If we tell the child what is wrong and then he corrects the mistakes, we may convince him and even ourselves that his relatively error-free final draft is actually his work. It is not. It is, at best, a sort of collaboration. This is not what schools have in mind when they set homework! Homework is designed to be the child's effort. To make finding the mistakes easier at first, use a system that lets the child know how many mistakes there are of each type. For example, you can jot "sp" in the margin if there is a word misspelt on that line. Then the child must use his brain to pinpoint the mistakes.

13 Descriptively Praise the child for finding errors. Be (and act) glad that he found the errors, rather than annoyed that he made the errors in the first place. Make it clear to him that the whole point of proof-reading is to discover errors, not to find that there are no errors.

14 If there is time, have your child proof-read his rough draft separately for each different type of error:

- Content – choice of topic
  - organisation of ideas
  - development of ideas
  - length
- Sentence construction
- Vocabulary
- Spelling
- Punctuation and capital letters
- Handwriting

Work through the essay, one aspect at a time, and at a leisurely pace, with the child doing the thinking, the explaining and the correcting.

15 If time is short, require the child to proof-read every piece of work he writes for at least one or two areas of accuracy. Concentrate on the areas that most need improvement.

16 Whilst your child is writing, either the rough draft or the final copy, do not correct or advise. This is his job to do on his own.

17 The final draft of homework should be executed in exactly the way the school requires. Most teachers have rules about how to write the heading, what and how to underline, whether Tipp-Ex™ is permitted, crossings out, inserts, etc. If a disagreement or question about acceptable presentation arises during Stages One or Three of the homework session, use your best judgement, rather than simply taking your child's word for it. Make a note to yourself to find out from the school exactly how they want it to be done.

18 When using the child's homework as the vehicle for teaching proof-reading, the parent should indicate, for the school's information, how much and what type of help or instruction the child received. Otherwise the child's teachers may be mystified or suspicious if his writing is suddenly improving. The best way to keep teachers informed is to send the rough draft back to school along with the final copy.

19 When there is enough time (usually weekends and holidays) do an exercise in which you or your child write a short paragraph purposefully containing many errors. Then have him practise finding the mistakes. This activity is fun and hones attention to detail.

20 Always end the session (or segment of the session) on an up note, with lots of Descriptive Praise.

21 Take a minute at the end of each homework session to jot down which proof-reading points have been revised and which need to be revised. It is easy to make the mistake of concentrating on certain aspects and ignoring other aspects.

Content, sentence construction and vocabulary

When your child's style is flowery, vague, garbled, padded or repetitive, do not let him attempt piece-meal corrections directly onto his rough draft. He will need to be taught how to simplify and clarify his points. This is best done on a new piece of blank paper, starting from scratch, rather than trying to fix the old work.

1   Put the essay or the paragraph in question completely away.
2   Have the child tell you what he is trying to say, while you write down each point in note form on individual Post-Its™, briefly, clearly and neatly.
3   Then he can rearrange the Post-Its™ until he is happy with the order in which he wants to make his points.
4   Finally, the child's job is to write one sentence for each of his points.

Over time, these steps will result in a cleaner, more mature style of expression. This technique also works whenever a child is stuck during Stage One of the homework. Even a child who can think of nothing to write can usually talk about the topic, if the parent asks leading questions.

Spelling

To help your child learn how to proof-read a piece of homework for spelling, make a list of all the words containing five or more letters that are spelled *correctly* in his essay. The child checks his work to see which words from his writing have been left off your list. To compare the words in his rough draft with those on your list, he has to pay attention to several pieces of information at the same time, which will eventually improve his working memory. As he identifies and corrects the misspelt words, you then add them to the list of correctly-spelled words. Seeing this list grow as he corrects his mistakes is highly motivating for most children, especially if you team it with lots of Descriptive Praise.

In addition, keep an ongoing list (which will change over time) of words that your child frequently misspells. Have him circle these words in his rough draft and then compare his spellings to the list.

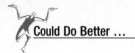

When there is time, have your child check the spelling of every word in his work that has more than five letters, or six or seven. First have the child go through and circle all those words, then go back and look them up.

When checking for spelling, have the child read the words out of context, for example by reading the piece of writing backwards, word by word. This will counter the natural tendency to see what one wants or expects to see, rather than what is really written on the page.

Take the time to help your child notice why he misspelt a word. Over time, this will give him the necessary tools to think about spelling as he proofreads (and eventually as he writes). Most children's spelling mistakes are caused by:

- missing out a silent letter (*anser* for *answer*, *bred* for *bread*)
- not understanding the rule for when to double the consonant before adding "ing" or "ed" and when not to (*cuting* for *cutting* and *slidding* for *sliding*)
- confusion between words that look or sound similar (*whent* looks like *when*, *except* sounds like *accept*)
- not remembering which vowel combinations makes the long-vowel sound in which words (e.g. *treet* for *treat*, *tale* for *tail*).
- writing all the right letters but in the wrong order (*gril* for *girl*, *brian* for *brain*)
- leaving off "ed" when writing in the past tense (*he walk* for *he walked*)
- confusing the spelling of words that sound identical but have different meangins (*to*, *too*, *two* and *there*, *their*, *they're*)
- attempting to spell words or syllables phonetically that are not spelled phonetically (*moove* for *move*, *shun* for *tion*)
- omitting the silent e that "makes the vowel say its name" (writing *hop* for *hope*) or over-generalising and adding a silent e where it serves no purpose (*hande* for *hand*).

Punctuation and capital letters

When proof-reading for punctuation, have the pupil proof-read in stages: first checking carefully for capitals at beginnings of sentences, next for full stops, question marks or exclamation points at the ends of sentences. Then have him proof-read for apostrophes, then for commas and finally for quotation marks.

Beware! Commas are very problematic, and acceptable usage can differ from school to school, even from teacher to teacher. So before asking your child to add or delete a comma, make sure that you know what rules he must abide by.

Handwriting

There is no point in correcting the handwriting of the rough draft because the child will not have been trying to write neatly. The best way to improve handwriting is to prepare for success by having a talk-through before the child starts writing the final copy: have him *show* you how he will form the letters which you know are problematic for him.

Proof-reading can be hell for children (and for parents) if we get annoyed at them for making "careless" mistakes. We need to remember that carelessness is often a learned response, the result of habitual avoidance or rushing. When we take the time to teach and train proof-reading as I have outlined in this chapter, the child's willingness to pay attention to details improves, as well as his ability to. Proof-reading may never become his favourite activity, but it can become much easier. You will see his confidence blossom as he starts to take pride in his work.

Chapter 14
Improving memory

Why memory matters

If your child does not easily remember what most other children of his age can easily remember, of course he will suffer academically. Many school subjects require ongoing memorisation, for example:

- English – spelling, rules of punctuation, parts of speech
- Mathematics – bonds, multiplication facts, procedures
- Sciences – procedures, definitions, formulae
- History – dates, causes and effects
- Foreign languages – vocabulary, verb endings, idioms
- Other subjects – specialised terminology

In addition, he may be less appealing as a friend if he is confused about what others his age take for granted. And he may have a harder time managing "real life", including keeping track of his belongings and remembering when he needs to be where. Difficulties in these areas rapidly erode a child's self-esteem. These are very important reasons for actively helping your child to improve his memory.

Parents often express bewilderment that the same child who can't seem to remember to put a full stop at the end of a sentence can have such an excellent memory for topics that he is passionate about. Unfortunately, his "specialist subject" is rarely a topic which will help him fulfil his academic potential. He may know, and want to tell you endlessly, all about every dinosaur ever discovered. Or he may be a walking encyclopaedia of all the minor characters in the Star Wars films. He may be able to discuss knowledgeably the strengths and weaknesses of every Pokemon™ or Yu-Gi-Oh!™ creature. Clearly this child has a well-functioning long-term memory for topics that sustain his interest.

So why does he have such difficulty remembering what we want him to remember? It is often because his short-term memory is relatively weak, immature, patchy, unreliable – and as yet untrained. Almost as soon as a piece of information enters his short-term memory, it starts to evaporate.

This is especially true if he:

- Has relatively weak auditory processing, by which we mean that he cannot easily listen and process the information that is coming in through his ears as quickly as the teacher is talking.
- Cannot yet read well enough to be able to take his attention off the process of decoding and put it on to the job of puzzling out the meaning of what he is reading.
- Is a kinaesthetic learner, and therefore very restless and distractible when he is expected to sit still and absorb information passively.
- Is emotionally under par because school is not a satisfying experience for him; he may be feeling anxious, embarrassed or resentful.
- Is pre-occupied with matters which seem far more important to him, such as who will play with him at break time or will his sandwich be soggy again today or will the teacher give him an annoyed look if he makes another mistake.
- Already has some confusion about the topic and therefore does not quite understand what the teacher is talking about
- Is not interested in the topic in the first place.

As we saw earlier, the short-term memory is the gateway into the long-term memory. If a fact or concept or skill falls out of the short-term memory every time we put it in there, it will not be in the brain long enough to be transferred into long-term storage. That is why a child can be told the same thing hundreds of times over many years (e.g. "Start sentences with capital letters", "Show your working out in maths", "The word *where* has an *h* in it") and still seem oblivious.

It should go without saying that it absolutely does not make sense to expect a child to memorise something before he understands it thoroughly. Proof of understanding is that your child can explain it to you:

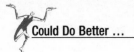

- correctly
- without any subtle prompts
- in his own words
- succinctly, without irrelevant or tangential additions.

Parents assume that this first step, that of making sure the child understands the material, will happen at school. When this consistently fails to happen, parents need to take charge, rather than letting the situation drift in the hopes that it will soon improve. By taking charge, I mean:

- educating yourself about what your child's problems are, what is causing the problems and what the solutions might be
- discussing with the school their understanding of the child's problems, suggesting ways to make learning easier for the child and monitoring closely what the school does about it and how
- during the homework session, breaking down the information into very small steps or micro-skills, and arranging for plenty of *successful repetition*.

Let us assume for now that your child understands the material that he is expected to remember. What often happens is that he will conscientiously try to memorise this week's spellings or dates or Geography definitions or French vocabulary. Even when his efforts are successful, the information has only entered his short-term memory. Unfortunately for him, the next week a whole new set of facts needs to be memorised. Last week's facts, unless they are rigorously reinforced, will soon fade from his short-term memory. That is why a child can know his eight times table or his spellings perfectly one day and not know them a few days or weeks later.

The solution to this problem of rapid forgetting is to make sure that the information enters the long-term memory, from which it can be retrieved at will with minimal prompting, even after a long time has elapsed.

Micro-skills training is all about *accurate memory storage*. We want the information or skills the child is practising to enter his brain in the correct form so that it will be retrieved in its correct form. So we must prevent the child from "practising" his mistakes.

Seven guiding principles follow which you can use to sharpen your child's short-term and long-term memory, leading to greater school success and increased confidence in every area of life. These principles are based on what researchers have discovered about how the brain works.

1. Cumulative review

One simple way to put the information into the long-term memory is to add an extra five minutes to each day's homework session. Use this extra time to review some of what was memorised in previous weeks. This is known as cumulative review. Of course, five minutes a day will not be enough time to cover all the previously-memorised material. But you will probably be amazed at just how much material you and your child can cover if you commit to this extra five minutes of review every day. That comes to 30 minutes a week, two hours a month and roughly five hours each term. That is more time than most children or teens spend reviewing past materials, unless they are revising for a specific exam. Think how accurate and quick your child could become at his times tables or spellings or quadratic equations or French idioms if he practises this much! And five extra minutes a day is practically painless.

I also recommend that you establish the habit of cumulative review at all weekends, half-terms and holidays, as well as on any days when your child's assigned work does not take up the full homework hour.

2. Over-learning

Keep revisiting the material to be learned until your child can rattle it off correctly, quickly, fluently, and with no prompts. Then revisit it some more! This is called over-learning, and it results in the information sinking into the long-term memory so deeply that the child will be able to recall and use most of it even under adverse circumstances, for example if he is tired, hungry, feeling unwell, over-excited or anxious.

The number of repetitions necessary for over-learning to take place is affected by numerous factors, both internal and external. When the material to be memorised is presented to the child through his strongest

channels, he will absorb it faster and more thoroughly, and he will be able to retrieve more of it more quickly. For most people, and this is especially true of most children who are experiencing school problems, the preferred cognitive channels are visual and kinaesthetic, that is, seeing and doing.

In addition, when a child is rested, relaxed, confident and engaged, his long-term memory stores and retrieves information more efficiently.

3. Association

We all memorise best and we all retrieve best when we can mentally attach a new fact to something we are already familiar with. All mnemonics work in this way. A mnemonic is a saying that helps us to recall information. For example, I can easily remember the fictitious name, "Roy G. Biv", and that gives me instant access to the colours of the rainbow in the correct order, which I certainly would not otherwise be able to reel off so fluently.

We can help our children to do the same thing. To start with, we can teach them to use all the mnemonics we already know, e.g.

- i before e except after c…
- 30 days hath September…
- <u>B</u>ig <u>e</u>lephants <u>c</u>an <u>a</u>lways <u>u</u>nderstand <u>s</u>mall <u>e</u>lephants (the first letters spell *because*)

We can also make a game of asking friends and extended family to teach us their favourite mnemonics.

Although we may not be consciously aware of the process, many times every day we use the power of what we already know to help us access or work out what we would find it difficult or impossible to "just remember". We know and use many tricks to help us remember. Let's say that you are helping your child to memorise the five times tables. He will find the process much easier if you teach him that the answers in the five times table always end in 0 or 5. This is something that we know but take for granted and rarely think about. But this fact will be very useful to your child as he is learning. Knowing this fact will help him at first to work out the right answer, rather than to impulsively blurt out his first guess. Later, when with repeated practise he is beginning to remember the answers, this fact about the 5 times table will enable him to self-check whatever answer he retrieves from his memory storage.

4. Meta-cognition

Meta-cognition is a word that has been coined quite recently. It is most often defined as "thinking about thinking" or "learning about how we learn". When we guide our children to look for, notice and use aide-memories and patterns, we are teaching them to think about how they think. Until recently, the assumption was that some people are good at learning (by which is usually meant understanding, remembering and using information or skills) and some people simply are not. We now know, thanks to a great deal of brain research, that our brains are extremely malleable and versatile, capable of learning how to learn.

One way we can help a child improve his ability to learn is to respond with a *diagnostic response* when he makes a mistake. A diagnostic response helps him to think about and understand why he made the mistake. Each time your child makes an impulsive or "careless" mistake during memorising or during homework, stop everything. He may be determined to keep going in order to get it over with, so you may even need to cover the page he is reading or writing on to prevent him from carrying on. Ask him to tell you what his mistake was and what he should have said or read or written instead. Give him a diagnostic response to help him to think about why he made the mistake.

For example, if you are helping your child to memorise the five times tables, you might ask "Five times five equals what?" and he might impulsively reply "Ten". Instead of saying "No!" or "Pay attention, for goodness sake!" or simply telling him the correct answer, a diagnostic response might be, "Maybe you thought I said 'plus' because 5 plus 5 is 10. Plus is adding. But I didn't ask you to add just now. What are you practising?" Once he understands the reason for his error, you can help him to sharpen his auditory attention to detail by asking him both questions at random; "5 + 5? 5 × 5? 5 × 5? 5 + 5?"

Be willing to take the time to Reflectively Listen about his frustration or about his anxiety that he will never get it right or his resentment of you for making him do something that feels emotionally uncomfortable.

5. Attempting to retrieve

For memorising to take place, it is not enough for the child simply to be exposed to the information, even if the exposure is very frequent. Think of all the bits of information that your child has heard or seen many, many times that have not yet sunk in. To be effective, the cumulative review must be active, not passive. In this context, "active" means that the child needs to try to dredge up the information from his memory, with fewer and fewer prompts. This is called attempting to retrieve.

When we attempt to retrieve the same piece of information many times, it is as if the brain notices that certain information keeps being needed. The brain comes to the logical conclusion that this information must be very important. So the brain takes the sensible precaution of storing the information in the long-term memory, from which it can be accessed easily and reliably.

Something very interesting happens within the brain when we spend even a small amount of time, on a *regular, frequent* basis, attempting to retrieve previously-learned material. The very act of attempting to retrieve bits of it seems to trigger the long-term memory into storing many *related* bits of information, even those bits that we did not review.

Spelling is a typical example of this phenomenon. If you and your child practise spelling for just five minutes a day, within a few weeks his ability to spell many new, unstudied words will improve significantly.

6. Repetition with variety

The more different ways a fact or skill is practised, the more solidly it will be imbedded in the long-term memory. Different bits of the information will be stored in different areas of the brain. Some of those areas will probably be more efficient at remembering, which will lessen the negative impact of the less efficient areas. In addition, practising the information in several different ways will make it easier for your child to transfer the learning to new situations. For example, when a child must memorise history dates, he needs, at the very minimum, to be able to answer both of these questions, e.g. "What year was the Great Fire of London?" as well as "What happened in 1666?"

Of course, amongst the many different ways that he will practise any bit of information to be memorised, we must include whatever ways the child will need to reproduce the information at school. For example:

- In the weekly French dictation test, the teacher probably reads out each sentence only once or twice, in a conversational tone and relatively quickly. At the beginning of the week, when the child is just becoming familiar with the new vocabulary, the parent may need to repeat each sentence or phrase very slowly several times, with exaggerated expression. But by the end of the week, the child needs to be practising his dictation the way it will happen at school. Otherwise he will not be adequately prepared.
- For a child with an unreliable memory to do well on a written spelling test, at home he must practise writing the words, not just spelling them aloud to you.
- Because one of the goals of spelling practice is for the child to spell correctly when he is composing essays and exam answers, he will need to practise his weekly spelling words by writing sentences. Otherwise, you may end up with a child who gets 100% on the spelling test but misspells the same words later the same day when he is writing a story.
- Going back to our question about the Great Fire of London, the child needs to be able not only to tell you the answer, but also to write the information in a full sentence which is correctly spelt, punctuated and capitalised. This takes practice!

7. Lengthening intervals

One more step is needed to achieve over-learning. As soon as the child can tell you the information correctly, quickly and fluently every day when you ask him, stop asking him every day and instead ask him every other day.

It will take him a few days or a week to regain the same speed and fluency as when you were asking him daily. Once he can recall the information easily when you are asking him every other day, move to asking him twice a week. Again, expect an initial drop in speed and fluency. Once the fluency has been re-established, ask for the information every week. When the response is quick and fluent again, ask every two weeks and then eventually every month for a few months. By then, the information will be securely locked in the long-term memory.

How to make memorising less arduous and possibly even fun

1   *Always* keep the micro-skills and memorising sessions short, a maximum of five to ten minutes (even if your child pleads for more, which may well happen if you follow these guidelines rigorously).

2   *Always* start with what you are sure the child knows. Easy questions first! This warms up his brain, as well as boosting his confidence.

3   Each micro-skill to be memorised needs to be broken down into bite-sized pieces.

4   *Always* respond positively to every correct answer:

- Smile
- Descriptively Praise, e.g.
    - "I remember when you didn't know that."
    - "Not one mistake!"
    - "You didn't rush. You thought about it carefully and your brain came up with the right answer."
    - "Three correct answers in a row!"
- Thumbs-up sign or other gesture of approval.

Phrase the questions differently each time, e.g.:

- 8 times 2 equals what?
- 2 times 8 is what?
- What is the product of 8 and 2?
- What is the answer if you multiply 8 and 2 together?
- How many lots of 2 are there in 16?
- What times 8 makes 16?

You may feel that you could not possibly dream up so many variations. With practice, however, you will surprise yourself.

6   Use a diagnostic response to help him understand his mistakes (see Meta-cognition, page 152).

7   Help your child come up with a way he can remember a fact or skill more easily (see Association, page 151).

8   Establish some new routines by doing them consistently, e.g.

- number bonds for five minutes each time the family gets in the car
- French verbs for five minutes at dinner time
- twenty correctly-spelled words while waiting in the check-out line at the supermarket
- five history dates while doing household chores together
- six science facts before the bedtime story.

9   We need to recognise that anxiety often lurks beneath reluctance, resistance, arguing, complaining and trying to rush to get it over with. We can address this anxiety with plenty of Descriptive Praise and Reflective Listening and by demonstrating the correct response.

Improving auditory memory

A. Echo exercise

This activity is appropriate for ages two through the teen years. It will help your child improve his:

- attention to auditory detail
- accuracy, fluency and reaction time of auditory processing
- ease of visualising what he hears
- categorising skills
- clarity of speech production
- ability to generalise to new situations
- understanding of the difference between a phrase and a sentence
- and, of course, confidence.

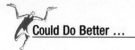

Remember to do this activity for no more than five or ten minutes at a time. Each time you do it, start at or near the beginning, even if your child mastered the first stages easily the last time. This will build confidence and ease him gently into the more difficult stages.

a Say "Repeat after me" or words to that effect. Frequently vary the wording of your instructions so that the child's brain has to think a bit, rather than simply respond automatically. For example, you could phrase it like this:

- "Say this word" or
- "Say this back to me" or
- "Echo what you hear me say."

b If necessary, start at the very beginning stage by asking your child to repeat back single words, first short ones and then longer words and eventually unfamiliar words.

c Once the child can correctly repeat back to you single words, with no hesitation, have him repeat short phrases (e.g. "a small kitten"), then longer and longer phrases (e.g. "the small white dog with the loud bark").

d Then have him echo complete sentences, at first short ones, then longer and longer, and finally sentences which include unfamiliar vocabulary.

e To improve your child's vocabulary, comprehension and fluency, have him practise paraphrasing each sentence in his own words.

f Next, have him repeat back to you a series of separate words, either related (e.g. cat, dog, monkey, giraffe) or unrelated (e.g. school, horse, grass, square). You may need to start with only three items in each series. But with practice, your child's memory will improve, and he will eventually be able to hold four or five unrelated words in his short-term memory, and even more if they are related in some way and if he understands how they are related.

g To help your child learn to categorise more precisely, ask him whether the words in the series are related or unrelated. If they are related, ask him to explain what those words have in common. When he tells you, require him to speak in full sentences.

h Then reverse the roles, so that your child takes a turn thinking up and saying the words, phrases, sentences and series of words for you to repeat. This step may be the most difficult for your child, but it is very important. Here your child is having to practise transferring what he has learned to a new and slightly more stressful context. This step will result in the most solid learning possible.

B Learning "by heart"

Every child will at various times in his school career be required to memorise poems, sayings, proverbs, prose passages, possibly a speech to be recited in assembly or a part in a school play.

Children with a history of under-achievement often find these tasks frustrating, anxiety-producing and ultimately demoralising. However, memorising long passages does not have to be a soul-destroying experience for your child (or for you). It can in fact be an enjoyable experience that boosts his morale, rather than tearing it down. To accomplish this you need to prepare for success *before* the school springs this task on him. You do this by training your child's brain in the skills needed for memorising long pieces.

Begin with rhyming poems of two to four lines. Move on to longer poems as the child's auditory memory improves.

Don't

- Don't expect your child to know how to memorise before you teach him how.
- Don't be annoyed or surprised by how quickly he forgets, by his confusion or by his reluctance to even try.

Do

1   Before even asking your child to start learning the piece, repeat it aloud yourself slowly, in a slightly louder than normal voice and with exaggerated expression, *at least ten times*. This first step is the most important, so do not rush it. Do it at the beginning of every memorising session, even if you think it is no longer necessary. We must not underestimate how quickly children with auditory weaknesses can forget and how easily their already fragile confidence can be shaken.

2 Ask questions to make sure that your child knows the meaning of all words, phrases and idioms contained in the piece. Once again, require him to answer in complete sentences, e.g.: "Clatter means a loud noise".

3 The next step is the same as Step 1 except that when you recite the poem you will omit the last word of each line, pausing expectantly as you smile at your child. For example,

Old King Cole was a merry old ……………,

And a merry old soul was ……………,

He called for his pipe and he called for his ……………,

And he called for his fiddlers ……………

If your child can chime in with the missing word, show that you are pleased. However, if after a pause of a few seconds at the end of each line he does not volunteer the missing word, then you supply the word and carry on reciting until you reach the end of the next line, where again you omit the last word and wait expectantly for your child to provide it.

This technique for eliciting a response is known as a "trailing statement". It has a huge advantage over questioning a child, which is the traditional way of finding out if a child remembers something. Questioning can make an anxious or confused or resentful child even more unconfident, hesitant or rebellious. But with a trailing statement, the parent has not put the child on the spot. You have not asked him directly what the missing word is. So if he is not yet able to say it, he does not feel like a failure, and he is not worrying about whether he is disappointing you.

Carry on with Step 3 as many times as necessary until he can confidently supply the last word of every line, with no prompts, hints or clues. In case you are concerned that your child might become bored, restless or frustrated, remember that he will be spending no more than five or ten minutes at a time on this activity.

4 When your child has mastered Step 3, move onto omitting the last two words of each line and pausing for your child to supply the missing words. Continue in this way, not rushing it, until he is reciting the whole poem. If you are willing to take the whole process this gradually, your child's confidence will blossom and he will start to get ahead of you, reciting more and more of the poem, not just the omitted words. Whenever that happens, give lots of Descriptive Praise, of course.

5   As soon as each verse of the poem is completely memorised, have him practise it:

- with expression
- with appropriate gestures and facial expressions
- standing in front of a mirror
- standing in front of family and friends
- by writing it in rough
- by writing it out neatly.

6   Once your child can recite the poem perfectly, with no prompts, do not assume that your job is finished. The poem is not yet embedded in his long-term memory. Over-learning is needed, which is accomplished by cumulative review and by attempts to retrieve at lengthening intervals. So several times a week, have the child recite some of his previously-learned poems or prose passages. Each month, add a new poem or prose passage.

What else should the child learn by heart?

- In preparation for the Christmas play (or any performance or special assembly), as early as October start having your child memorise the first stanza of all of the carols that he is likely to be hearing or singing. You can find out this information from the school. Familiarising your child well in advance will improve his interest in the proceedings, his focus, his willingness to join in, and his learning.

- Nursery rhymes are an important part of a child's general knowledge. One could even say that a knowledge of nursery rhymes and fairy tales forms the foundation of what is sometimes called "cultural literacy", a body of shared knowledge that enables a community to communicate effectively.

Most children, of course, learn nursery rhymes when they are very young, simply by hearing them many times, with absolutely no effort and no awareness that they are learning. But a child whose auditory memory is relatively immature will need extra help in this area, just as he will with family members' birthdays or his postcode or spelling the name of his school.

- If certain hymns are regularly sung or certain prayers regularly recited at religious services that your child attends, use the above strategies to help him first to understand and then to memorise the words. Do not assume that he already knows the words just because he has heard them many times. With children whose auditory memory is relatively poor, repeated exposure is probably not enough. It is as if the child's brain, through no fault of his own, is not easily switched on to listening-and-remembering mode. So first check whether your child can recite the prayers or sing the hymns with no prompts.

It is well worth taking the time and effort to help him understand and memorise the words. You will soon see him joining in more, looking more alert, being more interested in the concepts being talked about. Your strategies will have made the content of the services significantly more accessible and more relevant.

General knowledge

Many underachieving children and teens have huge gaps in their general knowledge, not just in their subject knowledge. Parents tend to accept their children as they are, and may not even notice these gaps. I frequently ask parents to jot down, over a period of a week or a month, all the information, not directly related to school work, that they notice their child is confused about or oblivious to.

Here is a small sampling of information that children and teenagers with auditory processing problems may have missed, taken from their parents' lists:

a   their complete address

b   the full names, in the right order, of all family members

c   the correct spelling of all the above

d   the birthdays of all family members

e   the surnames of their friends

f   the full names of their school and their siblings' schools, including correct spelling

g   the name of the train or underground station closest to their home, to school, to relatives and friends

h   what their relatives do for a living

i   the birthplaces of their parents

j   the home town of relatives they visit or write to

k   the months, the seasons and the days of the week, in the correct order

l   the dates of Christmas, Hallowe'en and Guy Fawkes' Night

m   the spelling of the prime minister's name

n   the difference between a town, a city, a county, a country and a continent

o   the names and approximate locations of continents and countries

p   the names of major cities in England and other countries

q   what was special about well-known historical figures

r   where their lungs are located

s   what wheat is

t   the characteristics of mammals

u   that the moon orbits around the Earth

v   (and in terms of life skills) how to operate an electric tin opener, Hoover™, dishwasher, washing machine, blender, juicer, microwave, etc.

Sometimes parents become defensive when faced with gaps in their children's general knowledge, asking me, "Why do these little facts matter?" These, and similar facts, are the foundation stones which children and teenagers need to have firmly in place in order to build a solid understanding of more complex academic subjects. General knowledge adds immeasurably to a person's social skills, and people may regard him as odd if he is ignorant of commonly known facts.

Most importantly, knowledge of these and similar facts helps children to understand their surroundings, to feel comfortable and to respond appropriately. The more easily children can navigate their world, the more actively and the more successfully they will participate. The more often children can respond successfully, the more alert and aware they become. Their listening skills and their memory will improve. They will be more able to fulfil their potential in every area of their lives. All this leads to increased motivation, self-reliance and self-confidence.

Some of this general knowledge is no longer taught at school; some is taught but not systematically. Possibly it was taught several years ago, way back in infant school, often quite sketchily, during brief discussions that your child may not have been really tuning in to. Probably most of the children in his class mastered these facts and concepts easily, so the teacher's attention moved swiftly on to the next steps of the curriculum, leaving some children behind. So if you are committed to making sure that your child knows these and other similar facts, you will need to teach him at home. Without a solid foundation of general knowledge, school work and real life will be far more confusing than they need to be.

The technique known as "trailing statements", which I have modelled at several points in this book, is very versatile and can be used whenever you want to help an impulsive, reluctant, immature, unconfident or anxious child to understand or notice or remember something. For example, you might weave trailing statements such as these into your everyday conversations:

- "Next month is …?"
- "Today is Saturday, so the day after tomorrow is …?"
- "The sun is really a star, and the Earth is a …?"
- "The Prime Minister is Tony …?"
- "My middle name is …?"
- "Granny used to work in a shop, but now she's a …?"
- "Guy Fawkes' Day is always in the month of …?"
- "The Thames River runs through the city of …?"
- "During World War Two, Winston Churchill was the …?"

If he does not respond within five or ten seconds, finish the statement yourself. Then immediately repeat the trailing statement for him to finish. When he can do this, have him say the complete sentence so that all the bits of the information are stored together in his long-term memory.

SECTION IV: Preparing for success by practising and providing a wholesome lifestyle

CHAPTER 15
Getting ready in the mornings – starting the day calmly

Morning Mayhem can be found in most families with children who are sensitive and intense or dreamy and slow-moving or disorganised and impulsive. Over the years, you may have become accustomed to your children's daily moans and complaints, their bickering over who gets the Mickey Mouse cup, their dawdling followed by a sudden panic over a mislaid exercise book, your own nagging and shouting in response. This daily dose of stress may seem inevitable, almost normal.

Morning Mayhem does not set children (or us!) up for a good day. Morning Mayhem is the opposite of preparing for success. We need to change our entire approach to this important piece of the day.

Calmer, easier, happier mornings are a vital ingredient of school success. It is extremely difficult for children to focus clearly and to confidently face the often heavy challenges of learning and behaving properly when they have recently been screaming or been screamed at, when they have been complaining and squabbling and blaming, when they have been hearing criticism and an impatient, annoyed tone of voice from parents.

We want to give our children the best start to their school day, so we need to do everything within our power to create a pleasant, calm, relaxed atmosphere in the mornings.

1   To maximise the likelihood that children will want to face each new day, we need to ensure that they regularly get enough sleep. See "Bedtimes, sleep and rest" (Chapter 22 in this section), on how to make this happen.

2   Tempers will be less frayed if there is not so much to do in the morning and more time to do it. So everything that can possibly be

done the evening before should be got out of the way. School uniform should be put ready but if there is none and you have a child who is fussy about clothes, have him choose his outfit the night before, and then do not let him change his mind the next morning.

3   Give yourself more time in the morning by waking up twenty minutes earlier. The increased peace of mind that comes from not having to rush around will more than make up for getting a bit less sleep.

4   Do not allow any screen before school. It makes dawdling worse, and it also tends to switch off the very brain functions that children need in order to get the most from school.

5   Children who are able to dress themselves need to dress themselves, every single day, even when you are in a hurry and even when they are whingeing about it. If, for a "quiet life" or for a quicker start to the day, you sometimes do for them some of the bits that they are able to do for themselves, you will be sending mixed messages which will reinforce the dawdling or moaning. Be warned that a child who has been used to having you perform this service for him may feel at first that he is being deprived of your love, care and attention when you tell him that it is now his job to dress himself. To ease him through this understandable reaction, stay with him while he dresses himself and Descriptively Praise all of his efforts, however feeble. This will, of course, take longer than if you help him to dress, but it is an investment that will pay off rapidly. Soon you will have a child who is proud of his new competence. This self-reliance and self-confidence will gradually spread to other areas of his life as well, as long as you do not jump in and do things for him that he can do for himself. As a bonus, you will be less annoyed, and you will soon have more time to get on with other things.

6   Most children wake up hungry. So a useful routine is to serve breakfast only after the children are completely dressed, hair brushed, beds made, pyjamas put away and school bags near the door. This rule helps children to stay focused on what they have to get done and eliminates most of the dawdling and staring into space or the sudden urge to build a Lego™ fort. It also eliminates most of our nagging!

7   Children's breakfasts need to be healthy. This sounds obvious, but many parents buy sugar-laden, high-fat breakfast foods because they say that those are the only foods that their children will eat in the mornings, and the parents do not, understandably, want their children going off to school on an empty stomach. Let's remember who is in charge. We know what is good for children, whereas they mostly know, and care about, what they like and don't like. Any child can get used to any food. Proof of this is that children all over the world accept and grow to like the foods that are regularly put in front of them, even foods that seem distinctly unappealing to people from a different culture. See "Mealtimes and Nutrition" (Chapter 16 in this section) for effective strategies that will help your children become healthier eaters.

8   As tempting as it is to rush around trying to get things done while the children are eating their breakfast, instead I ask you to sit down with them and chat. This is an excellent opportunity to preview their day, show an interest in their school lives, and Descriptively Praise their table manners, even if (or especially if!) you cannot find much to praise.

9   A significant minority of children and teenagers find school unrewarding. They do not feel successful, either academically or socially or both. So in the mornings, they are not looking forward to the day ahead. They may not even want to crawl out from under the duvet and face their family. When they do finally emerge, they are slow to get themselves ready, and are either dreamy or irritable, depending on their temperament type. Parental reminders do not seem to make much difference. Rather than our nagging, shouting or threatening consequences, a child like this needs a reason to get up and get going. He needs and deserves a more rewarding school experience. He needs parents who will be his advocates to make this happen.

CHAPTER 16

Mealtimes and nutrition

Many children with sensitive, intense, impulsive temperaments have a history of being faddy, fussy eaters with only a relatively narrow range of foods that they are willing to eat. Often entire food groups are rejected, most often vegetables and fruit. These children are easily turned off, sometimes even to the point of disgust, by the smell, texture or appearance of certain foods.

To compound the problem, these children often get hooked on and consume a lot of the very foods that have been found to contribute to their behaviour and learning problems:

- Sugar (in all its many disguises: not only sweets, but also biscuits, cakes, pies, breakfast cereals, jams, fruit yogurt, desserts and puddings, juice drinks and almost every food that comes in a box or a tin)
- Caffeine (this is in chocolate and in many fizzy drinks, as well, surprisingly, as in decaffeinated tea and coffee)
- Preservatives, emulsifiers, colourings, and other chemical additives
- Refined carbohydrates (in particular wheat)
- Dairy products.

Clinical studies as well as anecdotal evidence from parents show that these sensitive children are not just sensitive to their external environment. They are also unusually sensitive to their internal environment, namely what they eat. Some of these children have low-grade allergies, and many more have food intolerances, both of which can contribute to behavioural and learning problems as well as to the physical symptoms mentioned in Chapter 5.

As we have seen, concentration, learning, remembering and co-operative behaviour all require sustained focus. Many children with the most common school problems (difficulties with listening, learning, sitting still, co-operating quickly, staying on task, keeping friends) are very restless and fidgety. They distract themselves and their classmates from the task at hand by fiddling, poking and pulling, scratching, chewing their clothes and playing with any object in their vicinity. In many cases, the physical symptoms, the behaviour problems, the learning difficulties and the restlessness are vastly reduced, and the child seems calmer and better able to focus, when wheat, dairy, sugar, caffeine and many of the unnecessary additives are removed from the diet, except for a weekly treat.

Many parents are aware that sugar makes their child over-excited or tearful or irritable and easily frustrated. What is not so widely known is that in sensitive children sugar also adversely affects concentration, motivation, attention to detail, social awareness and short-term memory, all of which are essential school success skills.

Most parents know, in their hearts, that their children would be far better off without sugar or caffeine. But parents worry that their children would complain bitterly if they had to do without and would feel that life is terribly unfair. Healthy eating need not be experienced, by children or parents, as deprivation as long as you follow several guidelines:

- Do not have the foods that are not good for them in the house, so the visual temptation is removed.
- Do not eat or drink any forbidden foods in front of them.
- Descriptively Praise them for their willingness, co-operation, acceptance, etc.
- Reflectively Listen to how they may be feeling.
- Talk up the benefits of healthy food but do not lecture them about unhealthy food.
- Allow a weekly treat; make sure that this happens outside the home to keep the boundaries clear.
- Allow them to eat what the other children eat at parties.

Wheat and dairy products present a more difficult problem than sugar or caffeine for two reasons. One or both are ingredients in almost every prepared food. Also, wheat and dairy are both real foods (as opposed to sugar and caffeine, which function in the system more as strong chemicals than as food). So you may be concerned that your children

would be missing out nutritionally if wheat or dairy products were eliminated or significantly reduced. In particular, parents worry that without milk, children will not get enough calcium. Discuss this with your doctor, who, if he feels your child would benefit, will be able to tell you about alternatives to dairy, such as soya milk and soya yoghurt, originally developed for children with cow's milk allergies. You can ask to be referred a dietician or nutritionist.

Our job as parents is to provide the best quality food and to stay positive. We want to give our children the very best chance possible to do their best and be their best at home and at school, in terms of cognitive functioning and also co-operation, confidence, motivation, focus, problem-solving and perseverance.

Chapter 17
Quality Time

A great deal of misbehaviour, attention seeking and complaining about homework can be eliminated by giving children the positive attention they crave, need and deserve. One important way to do this is by arranging daily one-on-one "Quality Time", with no siblings in sight, no screen on in the background, your mobile phone switched off and no distractions.

It is very important that this Quality Time be *one* parent with *one* child. Even siblings who usually play well together need and deserve each parent's undivided attention. And for siblings who are in the habit of teasing, provoking or annoying each other, the time alone with one parent is bliss. For a short while they can relax and forget about the competition.

If the ideal of daily Quality Time seems impossible to achieve, be willing to start with very small chunks of time. Interestingly, once parents start dedicating ten or fifteen minutes a day to Quality Time with each child, the parents themselves soon grow to enjoy it, to look forward to it and to feel nourished by it. The parents then start planning for much longer chunks of Quality Time alone with each child at weekends and holidays. Here are some ways to get started:

- Sit with your children at *all* meal times, when they are a captive audience, and chat with each one for a few minutes in turn. Turn off the television, let the answering machine record the telephone messages and practise relaxing. It may not be easy at first. It may feel as if you are doing nothing, wasting time, being lazy or irresponsible, sitting around when you have a million and one things that need to get done. But you are doing something very important. You are building strong bonds and enhancing confidence and self-esteem, yours as well as theirs.

- At bedtime, spend five or ten minutes saying goodnight and chatting with each child separately. Make sure it is a positive experience, with no lecturing, criticism, reminders or exasperated tone of voice. If bedtime battles are getting you down and keeping you from staying positive, see Chapter 22 in this section.

- Whenever you are with just one child (in the car, on public transport, walking to school or to the shops, waiting to collect another child, waiting for an appointment, etc.) use this time to focus on enhancing and deepening your relationship with this child. Show an interest in whatever he is interested in, and also share your own enthusiasms.

- Even when you are busy getting things done, interrupt yourself and go to wherever your child is playing. Sit down near him for five or ten minutes and watch and chat. Rather than asking questions (which can be off-putting for the child and frustrating for the parent), share what you notice, throw in lots of Descriptive Praise, and elaborate on whatever he says.

- Wake your child on school mornings by sitting on his bed, stroking his hair or chatting about something pleasant. You can combine this with your morning cuppa and it makes for a much less grumpy start.

- Play a quick ten-minute game before the children are allowed their screen time.

- When your children are in front of a screen, sit down and watch a bit of whatever they are watching or playing. Even silent companionship can strengthen the bond and help a child to feel more accepted and appreciated.

- Take full advantage of a younger child's naptime, not just by catching up on the housework but by first playing for a while with the child who is awake.

- Get into the habit of requiring each child to help you, at least once a day, with part of a household task. Make sure to rotate the jobs. Be prepared for complaints of "It's not fair" or "But that's *your* job" in the first week or two. As you continue to insist, the moaning will soon fade away, and the children will even grow to enjoy these times, although they may never admit it. It is important to clearly label these times working together as Quality Time. This will help make it clear that you want the child with you for his company, not because you are trying to get out of doing some part of your job!

- Once a week, let each child stay up half an hour past his usual bedtime, and use this time to do something special together.

- Get into the habit of spending your Quality Time together in ways that do not cost money: card games, board games, puzzles, Lego™, drawing, crafts, making a special meal, throwing and catching a Frisbee™ (easier for a young or unco-ordinated child to handle than a ball), going for walks, having a picnic tea in the park. At first, self-conscious teenagers will probably turn up their noses at most of these "uncool" activities, so you need to persevere. Otherwise, you could easily get sucked into regularly taking them to the cinema, shopping or out for a meal for their Quality Time. All those activities cost money and can result in your feeling resentful and martyred when the children do not appreciate the expense.

- Seize every opportunity to Descriptively Praise. This, in and of itself, can turn an ordinary moment into a special moment.

To summarise: frequent, predictable, labelled Quality Time benefits all family members. The child's self-confidence, his enthusiasm for life, his willingness to tackle uncomfortable tasks and his motivation to please his parents all grow steadily when the most important people in his world are demonstrating an ongoing desire to spend time with him. For both parent and child, this Quality Time results in many pleasant memories which make it easier during any confrontation for the parent to remember the child's good qualities and for the child to remember the parent's good qualities. Everyone stays calmer.

CHAPTER 18

Screen time

The less time that children spend in front of a screen, the more co-operative and self-reliant they will become. Left to their own devices, however, many children, especially those with a difficult temperament or a subtle specific learning difficulty, will gravitate towards television, videos, computer games, Playstation™ and other console games, Game Boy™, games on mobile phones, e-mailing and texting their friends, "chatting" in chat rooms and surfing the Internet. Because it keeps them temporarily out of mischief and out of our hair, it is tempting to allow children to spend more time in front of a screen than is good for them. I am not suggesting for a moment that all screens should be banned, although those few brave families who have taken the bold step of eliminating television, videos and computer games completely have never regretted it. Nowadays, that would not appeal to many families. But most parents I talk to are very keen to get back in charge of the number of hours that their children and teenagers spend in front of a screen and also to get back in charge of the quality and suitability of what their children are being exposed to.

- Parents have reported many important benefits when children spend significantly less time in front of screens.
- Children learn to entertain themselves and are far more willing to.
- They are able to focus for longer, and they develop the patience to enjoy activities that challenge them intellectually.
- They ask for fewer toys and less junk food when they are exposed to fewer commercials.
- Physically they are more active, which improves muscle tone, posture, even digestion and sleep habits.
- They play more and talk more, which develops their social skills as well as their vocabulary and sentence construction.

- They put more energy and attention into all the other potentially enjoyable and rewarding activities that life has to offer: sports, practising musical instruments, hobbies, playing with friends, cuddling or chatting with parents, quiet games, even homework and revision!
- They are more willing to read – even those children who had previously never been seen with a book.
- They are more pleasant to be around. They are less grumpy, irritable or inclined to say "No", and they are more willing to do their homework and to help around the house.
- Siblings get on better, with less squabbling and sniping.
- When children have less exposure to on-screen aggression, intimidation, violence and destruction of property, their play gradually becomes less aggressive, less wild, even less competitive.
- There are huge improvements in many aspects of the children's school success skills.

To achieve these delightful results we need to be determined and strong and brave. Getting back in charge of our children's screen time means bucking the trend of the past fifty years. Based on the most up-to-date brain research, I advise that children up to the age of three years should have no exposure to screens. Between the ages of three and eight years old, it is recommended that children spend no more than a half an hour a day in front of a screen. From the age of eight onwards, all the way throughout adulthood, the limit should be an hour daily (except on special occasions, e.g. going to the cinema). And this means all screens combined, not an hour of videos, and another hour on the computer and another hour playing on the Game Boy! The daily hour of leisure screen time does not include the *legitimate* use of the computer for homework and projects. See Chapter 7 for strategies to halt the misuse of the computer during homework time.

We need to look carefully at the values imbedded in much of the electronic entertainment available today. In much of the programming, violence and inappropriate sexuality are portrayed as perfectly normal, even as humorous. Even if you limit your child's viewing to what is

widely considered to be age-appropriate fare, he will still be receiving many unwholesome messages, for example, that it is acceptable to lie as long as you don't get caught, that it is "uncool" to try hard at school, that parents and teachers are not worthy of respect, that siblings are nothing but a nuisance, and that rudeness is amusing.

Children who are sitting in front of a screen for a few hours a day are exposed to values like these not just once or twice in each hour but many, many times. It is like a slow, steady drip-feed. It is not surprising that the more children are exposed to these values, the more their own thoughts, beliefs and actions are influenced, and rarely for the better.

This is particularly true of the child who is unusually sensitive, intense and emotionally immature. Even when he has the intellectual maturity to understand that what he is watching is not reality, the fact is that aggressive, scary or sexually provocative images and story-lines will have a strong impact emotionally. Exposure to these themes can heighten his natural tendency to over-react, and can contribute to aggressive actions and thoughts, unwarranted anxiety or a fascination with the forbidden or dangerous.

We do not have much control over a lot of what happens to our children once they walk out of the front door. So it is all the more important that at home we focus constantly on creating an environment that reflects our values. We cannot completely eliminate all harmful influences, but we can radically curtail them and concentrate on substituting our own positive influences. Over time, this will result in children and teenagers who are more considerate, more polite, more focused when it comes to schoolwork, more interested in others and more co-operative – in short, children who are growing up with more wholesome values.

Here are some tried and tested ways of reducing children's screen time and also of getting back in charge so that you, the adults, are the ones who decide what your children will be exposed to. You can expect your children to resist this plan at first, although parents are universally surprised and delighted to see how quickly children (and even teenagers!) make the adjustment. The trick is to *completely* stop nagging, repeating, reminding, cajoling, lecturing and predicting a dire future. Instead, take action.

1 Get all electronics out of the children's bedrooms and into the public, often-frequented parts of the house.

2 Have only one television set in the house, only one Playstation, only one Game Boy and only one computer for the children. This way it will be easier for you to keep track of who is doing what for how long on which machine. And each child will have less access to the electronics. Other activities will suddenly start to seem more appealing.

3 Allow screen use only on certain days. For many families it works very well to have Monday through Thursday as screen-free days so that children can concentrate in the evenings on their homework. Another solution that works for some families is "one day on, one day off".

4 Require all tasks that the child might try to avoid or to rush through to be completed *to your satisfaction* before any screens can be switched on. The list of such tasks usually includes homework, reading, projects, memorising and revision, but can also be extended to include walking the dog, feeding the guinea pig, tidying their bedrooms, helping prepare the evening meal. For some children, even having a bath goes on this list.

5 Make screen time a reward for small daily successes: putting litter in the bin, remembering to bring home the homework diary, not teasing the baby, not arguing. At first you may need to keep all hand-held electronic games and possibly also the remotes in your possession, except when the child has earned his reward.

6 Sit down with your children weekly or every few days and help them plan what they will watch and when they will each have their turns on the computer. The secret to making this work is to give them plenty of time to choose carefully, and then do not let them change their choices. Have them make a chart so that nothing is left to imperfect memories.

7 Every day, sit down next to your child and watch some of what he is watching. You will probably be appalled at the values he is being exposed to. This will strengthen your determination to get back in charge!

8 Do not fall into the trap of turning the television on so that you can get some peace and quiet. Children and teenagers knew how to amuse themselves for thousands of years before screens came along! Some children are so used to being entertained that they have never learned to play by themselves. These children soon learn how, once they realise that sitting in front of a screen is now strictly rationed. Children with subtle specific learning difficulties may have problems learning how to play independently and may even need to be taught how (see Chapter 20 in this section).

9 Make a rule for the children that they must ask a parent *each time* they want some screen time. And make a rule for yourself that you will answer positively. You can say "Yes, as soon as you show me your completed homework" or "Yes, once your list is all ticked" or words to that effect. If you say "No" or give them a mini-lecture about the evils of television and the joys of fresh air or reading, you will be reinforcing their initial feeling of deprivation.

10 Keep the television and computer in a cupboard or covered by a piece of cloth so that they are not continually beckoning.

11 Lead by example. When your children are in the house or garden do not give in to the temptation to sit in front of a screen as a way of relaxing. Wait until they are in bed and asleep before you switch on.

12 Do not have any screens on during meals.

13 Wean children off the mistaken belief that they cannot survive the tedium of a car or train journey without their Game Boy. Instead they can chat, sing and play games (by themselves or with you) or stare out of the window and daydream.

All the above suggestions may sound hopelessly old-fashioned and unworkable. They have all been proven to work!

If you think your child would object to this healthier lifestyle, you're right; he probably will object, at first. However, if you stand firm and stay positive, with no nagging or lecturing, the natural ability of all children to create their own entertainment will resurface. And the whole family will reap the benefits.

Chapter 19

Keeping belongings tidy and helping with household tasks

The more effort we put into training our children to be self-reliant, the more confident, motivated and co-operative they will become. The more consistently we train our children to be helpful, the more respectful, appreciative and responsible they will become. This maturity and self-reliance starts at home and will soon spread to school and to other social situations.

Training means establishing habits, and training is one of our most important, and most rewarding, jobs as parents.

The key to training a child to be self-reliant is insisting and WAITING, instead of giving in and doing it for him, or repeating, reminding and justifying, instead of shouting or smacking. We need to insist with friendliness, not with irritation. It is not the child's fault that in the past we did too much for him and allowed him to drift into the habit of expecting to be waited on.

The first household task that children are generally expected to be responsible for is putting away their toys after playing. Learning to take good care of one's possessions is a necessary skill for school success.

We can make learning how to be organised much less daunting, much quicker and easier, by investing some time and effort in several useful strategies. To begin, we will need to weed out all the out-grown or broken equipment, books, games and toys so that it becomes easier for the child to know and value what he has. If you take your child with you when you drop off the unwanted items at the charity shop, he will be learning important lessons about sharing and recycling.

After this weeding, your child will probably still have more sports equipment, electronic gadgets, clothes, toys, books, games, CDs and videos

than there is adequate space for. Box up most of them and put them out of sight. When you bring one of these boxes out again after a few weeks or months, the contents will be "new" again, fresh and exciting. This way your child's natural craving for stimulation and novelty can be satisfied without your feeling that you have to keep buying him new things.

- In some families one box is brought out with great ceremony, and another box put away, every weekend or on the first of each month.
- Other families do a straight exchange: the child may ask for an item from a box at any time, but he needs to replace it with something that is currently in his room.
- Many families allow the children to play for an hour or two with one of the stored toys as a reward for small improvements in co-operation.

To help children get into the habit of putting things back in the right place, we need to designate a specific, easily accessible place for all items. Labelling shelves and containers clearly (with symbols for non-readers) makes the child's job much easier. Children and teenagers will be more able, and therefore more willing, to unload the dishwasher or help put away the shopping when they can check the labels on shelves to see what goes where.

We want the child's brain to register tidiness and organisation as the norm. That can only begin to happen if your child is used to seeing his room tidy. So we need to make sure the clutter and mess never build up. An extremely effective way to achieve this is to have a five-minute tidying-up time before each meal and before each day's screen-time.

One of the many advantages of having fewer items available is that the child tends to concentrate on each one for longer. This improves attention span, imagination, and the ability to tolerate frustration, as well as problem-solving skills and perseverance. These are all very important school success skills that need to be learnt at home. Only then can he take them with him in his "tool kit" as he ventures forth into the larger world of school, Cubs, karate lessons, friends' homes, etc.

Chapter 20

Playing independently

When children are in the habit of playing alone or entertaining themselves for a good chunk of time every day, they become significantly more self-reliant and more skilled at problem-solving. They are less demanding and irritable. One of the most important school success skills that a child needs to learn is how to occupy himself for longer and longer stretches of time, without needing much adult input to keep him focused. Most children will not be able to do this well at school unless they are regularly practising this skill at home.

Some children are very capable of playing by themselves, but they only do it when they choose to. We need to help these children get into the habit of occupying themselves not only when they feel like it but also when the parents or childminder are too busy or stressed to interact with them positively, as well as when no playmates are available. The way to forge this habit is to designate a playing-quietly-in-your-room time every single day, and insist on it. Siblings should be in separate rooms for this.

It is tempting to park a habitually noisy or demanding child in front of a screen so that you can have some peace and quiet to get your chores done. But when we take the easy way out the child will not be practising the school success skills that can help him to fulfil his potential, to become more mature and more socially aware and, most importantly, to build his confidence and self-esteem.

Often this child spends a great deal of his non-screen free time in wild, noisy play, which often includes doing things he has been told many times not to do, or hanging around the adults or his siblings, trying to get their attention by increasingly irritating means. The child I am describing is often a restless and distractible child with immature fine-motor skills. He assumes that quiet, sitting-down activities will be "boring" even

before he tries them. He does not realise, of course, that he finds certain activities boring because he is not yet good at them and so derives very little satisfaction from them. Because he avoids these activities whenever possible, he rarely "practises" them so he does not get better at them. When he is expected, at school, to sit quietly and concentrate, he finds it very difficult, even physically uncomfortable. He will probably get reprimanded for not paying attention. The more he is criticised or spoken to in an impatient, irritated way, the more reluctant, resistant and possibly even rebellious he may become. Meanwhile, he is still not *learning how* to sit still and concentrate. This is a vicious circle which only parents can reverse. Most teachers are not equipped to teach children how to be self-reliant, and it is not their job.

Often (but not always), the child who is not good at playing quietly by himself is significantly or slightly behind his peers in reading, writing and numeracy, as well as in mature behaviour and social skills. Sometimes a decision is reached, after much deliberation, to have an immature, inattentive, very active child repeat the year, in the hopes that an additional year of maturity will enable him to focus better on learning, as well as to be less reactive or aggressive with his peers. The assumption, or hope, is that an extra year of exposure to the same facts, skills and classroom routines will result in more solid learning, greater confidence and improved behaviour.

Occasionally this plan unfolds smoothly and the repeated year is a success. But more often than not, the child will *still* be immature relative to his peers, exhibiting most of the previous year's academic, behavioural and social problems, with perhaps a slight improvement. Repeating the year can be part of a successful solution, but it must not be seen as the whole solution. This child will still need to be *taught how* to do what his peers can do quite naturally: sit and listen, focus for increasing lengths of time and think before he speaks. Although time does bring added maturity, rarely does a child with this distractible, highly active, intense temperament simply outgrow his distaste for quiet, focused activities (unless he is focusing on a screen).

The parents of this child need to accept, I believe, that they will have to *teach him how* to play (and then work) quietly and independently. This can usually be accomplished in a few weeks if you are willing to devote 10–20 minutes to it on most days. Here is how to begin:

Every day, put out on the floor a game that one person can play alone, or a puzzle, paper and coloured pencils, some books, toy cars, blocks, Lego™, etc. Sit on the floor and start playing by yourself, *without* inviting the child over. Talk to yourself *out loud*, with interest and enthusiasm in your voice, about whatever you are doing, e.g. "I've drawn a great, big yellow sun" or "This car needs some petrol. I'm going to pretend that this shoe is the petrol station". Wait patiently for your child to wander over when he becomes curious or wants your attention.

Talk with great enthusiasm about whatever your child does in relation to the activity, no matter how minimal:

> "You've chosen the whale book."
> "That looks like a castle you're building. Are those guys going to be knights?"
> "Maybe your car needs petrol as well."

The purpose here is not to play *with* your child. That is an activity suited to Quality Time (see Chapter 17). Our aim here is to:

- demonstrate how to play by oneself
- show by our enthusiasm that playing by oneself is fun
- Descriptively Praise him for every tiny step towards quiet independent play.

If your child asks you to draw or make something for him, don't. That would shift the focus back on to you as the entertainer. It could also reinforce his belief that he cannot do these things well enough. If you keep Descriptively Praising his efforts, after the initial grumbling or tears he will become more and more self-reliant and self-confident. He will start to find enjoyment in solitary play.

You may have a child who from a young age has just wanted to crash his toy cars together, smash down towers of blocks, draw pictures of battles or pretend he is killing bad guys or capturing enemies. Some of this is absolutely normal, especially for boys. However, a pre-occupation with aggression or violence is particularly common amongst boys with

sensitive, intense, impulsive temperaments, especially when they have built up a lot of anger, due to frequent criticism at home or at school. Regardless of the cause, a child with this tendency needs to learn to find satisfaction in non-aggressive pursuits as well.

So when you are sitting next to him playing, make a rule that there is to be no killing or dying, no crashes or explosions. Prepare for success by having several talk-throughs about this each day, asking your child the rule, rather than telling him. At first it may be quite difficult for this child to enjoy a game or activity that does not involve some imaginary violence or aggression. When he forgets the rule and drifts back to aggressive play, as he certainly will at first, just have him do an Action Replay (see Chapter 8). If you are consistent, it will not be too long before he builds up a tolerance for, and eventually even a liking for, activities that he previously dismissed as boring.

Make sure to keep varying the items you bring out so that your child becomes skilled at and comfortable with a wide range of quiet, solitary activities. Don't bring out the same activity more than once a week, even if he pleads. If he wants it enough, he will eventually start playing with it when you are not around, and that is what we are aiming for.

Children are far more likely to imitate the actions and attitudes of the same-gender parent. This can be a problem for boys, who often spend much more time with their mothers than with their fathers. To partially redress the balance, make sure that at weekends and on holidays the father or another male relative or friend of the family is the person doing the self-reliance training.

Chapter 21
Exercise

When children can let off steam out-of-doors every day, they do less whingeing, crying and answering back. They concentrate better, are less moody and more cheerful, and they have a higher tolerance for frustration. These are all qualities that are needed for school success, as well as for managing "real life" more successfully. Some children, particularly boys and particularly those with a difficult temperament, seem to have a much greater need than other children for lots of physical activity. This may feel too inconvenient to arrange, but it is an investment that pays off in calmer, more co-operative children who will be able to focus, persevere and do their best, both at school, at homework time and at all other times. Here are some examples of how parents have managed to build in physical activity on a daily basis:

- To release excess energy, take the children to the park every day for an hour after school, regardless of the weather.
- Have them bounce on a mini-trampoline for twenty minutes before they can go on the computer.
- Play ball with the children in the garden, even in the winter, even in the dark.
- When outdoor play is just not possible, parents need to set aside a certain time each day for movement activities, such as star jumps, rough-and-tumble, dancing, stretching exercises, practising karate or punching a home-made punch bag.

Physical activity confers numerous benefits, all of which indirectly but significantly help a child to fulfil his academic potential.

- A child who gets plenty of exercise every day goes to sleep more easily and sleeps more soundly, and therefore wakes more truly rested and refreshed. He is less irritable, less easily upset, more able to stay on task and to remember what is expected of him.

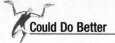

- Vigorous physical activity also seems to help resistant, reluctant learners to "burn off" some of their anger and anxiety about schoolwork and homework.
- Fidgety, restless, impulsive children become significantly calmer and less "hyper" when they have vigorous exercise every day. This calmness enables them to focus better and for longer.

Chapter 22

Bedtimes, sleep and rest

When children and teenagers get enough sleep, they do a better job on their homework, they "listen to reason" more, they argue and complain less, they accept limits more readily, and they even squabble less with their siblings. This especially applies to children with sensitive, intense, impulsive temperaments.

Unfortunately, getting enough sleep almost always entails a much earlier bedtime than a child would naturally choose for himself. Children need more sleep than they want. Unless we are clear and consistent about bedtime rules and routines, numerous problems can arise:

- The child may be unbearably slow at getting ready for bed, using clever delaying tactics or simply getting distracted.
- He may believe that he should not have to go to bed because he does not feel tired.
- He may refuse to go to bed or do so only under duress, with much arguing, crying, shouting or complaining.
- Once he is finally in bed and the light has been turned off, he may keep getting out of bed, either to come to you or just to play or go on reading in his room.
- He may stay in his bed but keep crying or shouting for you.
- He may work himself up into a genuine fear of the dark, or of monsters, burglars, etc. and become convinced that he cannot go to sleep unless a parent stays with him or he sleeps in the parents' bed.
- He may be so fixated on a certain bedtime routine that any deviation upsets him and delays his settling.

These behaviours are particularly upsetting because they come at the end of a long day, when the parent is worn out and desperately looking forward to a bit of off-duty time.

Here are a number of successful strategies. Some are more relevant for younger children, some for older children and teenagers. The more of these strategies you put into place, the sooner your children and teens will get into the healthy habit of going to bed at the right time with a minimum of fuss, falling asleep quickly and staying asleep until morning. This will improve co-operation during the school day, at homework time and of course during the rest of the day.

Research indicates that the experiences of the final three-quarters of an hour before one falls asleep have a huge impact on our unconscious, affecting the quality of our sleep, the tone of our dreams, even the mood with which we face the next day.

1 Four or five times during the day, take a few minutes to do a preparing for success talk-through: discuss the new rules and routines with your child, not by telling or lecturing, but by asking him what he will and will not do at bedtime and what you will and will not do. Expect your teenager to complain bitterly that you are the strictest parents in the world and that all his friends are allowed to stay up as late as they want.

2 Reflectively Listen to your child about his fears and worries during the day only, not at bedtime or in the night.

3 Never use bed as a punishment, or even threaten it. We want to foster a positive, or at least neutral, feeling about bedtime.

4 Play with your child for a half-hour each afternoon or evening so that he does not feel the need to prolong the bedtime routine as a way of getting your attention.

5 Allow no snacks after supper is over. It is easier to get to sleep and to stay asleep if the last meal is mostly digested.

6 Eliminate sugary foods so that the child is not "hyped up" and "wired" at bedtime.

7 Drastically reduce screen time so that children are more active and consequently more tired by the end of the day.

8 During the hour before the bedtime routine begins, ban all screen or noisy or exciting games. Substitute more relaxing activities to help your child wind down.

9 If you have a young child who is attached to a special blanket or soft toy, make sure that it always stays on the bed. That will make his bed more inviting. This rule will also help your child learn to self-soothe during the day, when his comfort object is not accessible.

10 Parents need to alternate being in charge of the bedtime routine so that the child does not become dependent on one parent.

11 Start the bedtime routine early, so that you are not stressed and so that you are not tempted to hurry the children. Slow down and try to enjoy being with your children. Descriptively Praise every few minutes to help all of you stay focused on the positive.

12 Follow the same routine every evening.

13 Do not let your child leave his reading homework until bedtime. He needs to be fresh and alert to do his best.

14 Keep all lights very dim during the bedtime routine; this helps children's brains to begin switching off.

15 Keep all screens and loud music off during the bedtime routine; this also helps children to gradually unwind.

16 Do not answer the telephone or even look at a new text message during the bedtime routine; give the children your full attention. Everything will go more smoothly and quickly if you do.

17 Do not stay in the bedroom until your child falls asleep or he will become dependent on it. A child who is very anxious or inflexible may need to be weaned off this dependence on your presence in several small stages. If necessary, start by sitting in a chair near the bed (but not on the bed) until he is almost asleep. Every day move your chair a bit farther away from the bed and closer to the door. By the time you are sitting outside his room and he can no longer see or hear you, he will have learned how to get to sleep without help. Remember to Descriptively Praise every step in the right direction because going to sleep on his own can be scary proposition at first for a sensitive, intense or unconfident child.

18 If your child gets out of bed after lights out, *silently and swiftly* take him back to bed, avoiding eye contact as much as possible, as many times as necessary. Once the child is lying down again and not fussing, then and only then give a smile and a short Descriptive

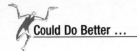

Praise. When children experience, over a few weeks, that getting out of bed is no longer rewarding, they soon drop the habit. Their real need for sleep takes over.

19 If your child often cries or shouts for you from the bed (but without getting up), have many talk-throughs during the day and before every bedtime about what will happen. He needs to know that you will check on him after lights out. After leaving the room, wait about five minutes, then go back into his room for just a moment, only long enough to re-settle him if necessary and give some brief Descriptive Praise, nothing else. Then leave the room again. Next, wait about ten minutes and do the same thing. Carry on with this technique, gradually lengthening the time between your visits to his room. This technique will transform his experience of bedtime.

20 Do not allow children or teenagers to stay up past their bedtime to finish homework or projects or to squeeze in some last-minute revision. That would de-stabilise their routines and unintentionally send a message of panic. If they are really so very keen to get more work done, they can always get up earlier the following morning. They are rarely that keen.

21 Even a child who does not need a lot of sleep still needs plenty of rest, although he may fight it. Allow older children and teenagers to read or draw in bed if they are not yet tired, but do not deviate from the bedtime you have set.

22 Older children and teenagers, who are no longer put to bed by a parent, still appreciate and are calmed by a short, loving saying-goodnight ritual. Don't skip this, even if you are annoyed with your child because of rule-breaking earlier in the day.

23 On non-school nights allow older children and teenagers to stay up a maximum of one hour later than their usual bedtime. You do not want to risk disrupting the healthy rhythms you have established, which are so important for school success and general cheerfulness.

24 Remember to Descriptively Praise everything that is going right at each stage of the bedtime routine.

CHAPTER 23
Where to go from here

Once you start putting the School Success Skills programme into practice, very quickly you will notice small, subtle improvements in attitude, attention span and learning – often within days, certainly within weeks. As with practising any new routine or learning any new skill, the first few weeks are the hardest. But if you stick with this plan, within a few short months you will see significant progress. For some children, the School Success Skills programme will be all that is needed to get their learning and their self-confidence back on track.

For other children, usually those with more severe problems, more help may be necessary. When looking for help from professionals, parents are easily confused because there are many different ways that a child with school problems can be assessed and helped, some of them well-known and widely respected, others less well understood and as yet less popular. In order to help a child fulfil his potential, parents can pursue remedial tutoring, conventional therapies, alternative treatments and medical interventions. For almost every approach you choose to explore, you will discover some parents who found it very helpful for their child and some parents who did not see much improvement.

From my own investigations, I have experienced that all interventions work better when parents commit to establishing enjoyable and productive homework habits. So whichever additional approach you may choose to explore, give it a fighting chance to make a real difference to your child's life. Persevere with this School Success plan. If you are wondering whether there might be any combatibility between this programme and any other approach, simply show this book to the professionals, and they will advise you.

I am hoping that by now you are feeling empowered to get back in charge of your children's learning and behaviour. Remember:

> **Our children's education is far too important to leave up to the schools.**

So get started. It will not always be plain sailing. But everything – homework, family life and parenting – will become *calmer, easier, and happier* the more positive, firm and consistent you remain. As you put the School Success Skills programme into practice for one hour every day, you will be helping your child to fulfil his potential, an invaluable gift that all parents want to give their child.

Appendix A

This list of 220 words, prepared by E.W. Dolch, makes up from 50 to 75 per cent of all reading matter, exclusive of proper names. If your child can read and spell these words correctly, with ease and speed, all schoolwork and reading will become much easier and more enjoyable!

a	can	clean	fast	got
about	because	cold	find	green
after	been	come	first	grow
again	before	could	fly	had
all	best	cut	five	has
always	better	did	for	have
am	big	do	found	he
an	black	does	four	help
and	blue	done	from	her
any	both	don't	full	here
are	bring	down	funny	him
around	brown	draw	gave	his
as	but	drink	get	hold
ask	buy	eat	give	hot
at	by	eight	go	how
ate	call	every	goes	hurt
away	came	fall	going	I
be	carry	far	good	if

in	myself	red	thank	want
into	never	ride	that	warm
is	new	right	the	was
it	no	round	their	wash
its	now	run	them	we
jump	of	said	then	well
just	off	saw	there	went
keep	old	say	these	were
kind	on	see	they	what
know	once	seven	think	when
laugh	one	shall	this	where
let	only	she	those	which
light	open	show	three	white
like	or	sing	to	who
little	our	sit	today	why
live	out	six	together	will
long	over	sleep	too	wish
look	own	small	try	with
made	pick	so	two	work
make	play	some	under	would
many	please	soon	up	write
may	pretty	start	upon	yellow
me	pull	stop	us	yes
much	put	take	use	you
must	ran	tell	very	your
my	read	ten	walk	

Appendix B

Please refer to The New Learning Centre's website (www.tnlc.info) for our ever-expanding list of useful resources (organisations, programmes, professionals and publications), arranged by category, e.g.:

Advocacy	Depression
Aggression	Dictionaries
Alternative therapies and treatments	Differentiation
Anxiety	Dyslexia
Asperger Syndrome	Dyspraxia
Attention	Easy reads (high interest, low skill)
Atypical learning styles	Educational psychologists
Autism	Handwriting
Behaviour	Homework
Bi-polar disorder	Hyperactivity
Bullying	Language
Classroom behaviour	Learning style
Comprehension	Lifestyle
Computers	Listening
Communication	Literacy
Consistency	Mathematics
Conventional therapies and treatments	Medical interventions
Cooperation	Memory
Decoding	Motivation

Books by Noël Janis-Norton, published by Barrington Stoke:

Can't Smack? Won't Smack? (for parents)
New ways that work better to bring harmony to families – And why the old ways don't work
In Step with Your Class (for teachers)
Managing behaviour in an inclusive classroom
Learning to Listen, Listening to Learn (for teachers)
Using language to enhance learning and behaviour in the inclusive classroom